ELEMENTS OF ANTHROPOLOGY
A Series of Introductions

The Origin and Evolution of Language

Brian Stross
University of Texas

wcb

WM. C. BROWN COMPANY PUBLISHERS
Dubuque, Iowa

ANTHROPOLOGY SERIES

Consulting Editors
Frank Johnston
University of Pennsylvania

Henry Selby
Temple University

Contents

Preface

Humans seem almost characteristically to have a consuming interest in the origins of things, whether it be the origin of the universe, the origin of life, the origin of man, or the origin of language. The fact that we can imagine a succession of forms through time, an evolution as it were, has always tantalized us with the hope that uncovering the correct sequences and fitting them into a framework of theories about process or change might lead to the original form from which all others ultimately developed. This interest in origins is reflected in the nearly universal cultural phenomenon of creation myths, both "primitive" and "scientific."

The search for origins—a diachronic view of structure—proceeds from and depends upon another generally human and characteristically scientific endeavor: discerning patterns or regularities underlying the often seemingly unorganized data of experience, a synchronic view of structure. These regularities support inferences about the structuring of forms and about their relationships with other forms.

Languages in this sense are forms. They are complex systems of communication, structured internally by identifiable units on several levels of organization; units that are interrelated within and between levels. Language systems can also be thought of as structured externally as well. That is, they are themselves units or subsystems of more inclusive cultural systems and interact with other subsystems in potentially specifiable ways. Surely it is natural, then, not only to ask how, when, and where languages originated and how they have changed through time, but also to ask the methodologically prior questions: what is the nature of language, and how does it articulate with other cultural subsystems of communication? These questions cannot be answered fully or even adequately today, but they provide a useful orientation for approaching an understanding of language in its sociocultural context, the primary goal of linguistic anthropology. Even though we have no way of verifying hypotheses concerning the structure and functions of the "first language," the search for a plausible reconstruction is justified both heuristically and as one of several possible guidelines for judging the relevance of research.

Rather than being simply a composite creation myth, this volume is intended also as an introduction to some of the concepts, methods, and results that have contributed to present conceptions of the role of language in society. As a means to both these ends, studies of animal communication systems, neurolinguistics, language acquisition, and language universals are viewed as windows into the past. From all these descriptive research areas come classifications of things and events which can be ordered sequentially and sometimes in terms of chronological priority. Further triangulations on the past come from a consideration of some more explicitly diachronic topics, such as the comparative method, internal reconstruction, and lexicostatistics.

1 | The Nature of Language

Numerous and persistent reports of hairy manlike monsters have come from many parts of the globe. Few zoologists, however, take them seriously. Most of the alleged sightings in recent years have come from California and the Pacific Northwest, where this creature is known variously as Sasquatch, Bigfoot, and Omah. Reported descriptions indicate that these Sasquatches are seasonally nomadic, primarily vegetarian, fleet of foot, and smelly. They move about alone or in small family groups and communicate vocally in strange sounding high-pitched whistles. Some observers suggest that Sasquatch may represent the last vestiges of a Neanderthal population, surviving in out-of-the-way places for the past fifty thousand years, isolated by their nocturnal habits from modern man. To the extent that such a creature might reflect an earlier stage of evolution, adequate verification of its existence and description of its communicative habits would be of immense interest to anyone seeking knowledge about the origin and evolution of human language.

In the absence of acceptable documentation and descriptions of the Sasquatch and similar quasi-humans, we are restricted to a known world containing only human communities that are fully human. And the languages spoken in all known human groups are fully languages. A century ago there were in the neighborhood of five thousand languages in the world (estimates range from three thousand to seven thousand). Many have become extinct since then, but one suspects that at least three thousand separate languages are still spoken today. The world's languages are structurally and functionally diverse, but at the same time they share many formal and substantive characteristics, which allows us to use the generic term "language" in referring to those things shared by all languages.

Some characteristics—such as gender distinctions in pronouns which we find in Spanish, German, Chinook, English, and many others—are shared by several languages, but not all, so they are not universal. Nonuniversal similarities and differences among languages can be used to classify them in various ways. A *genetic* classification groups languages on the basis of similarities due to common retention of ancestral features. An *areal* classification utilizes similarities brought about by contact and borrowing (i.e., diffusion). A third sort of classification groups languages on the basis of *typological* similarities that are independent of historical connections.

One approach to language origins and evolution is to equate groupings in a language classification with evolutionary stages. Another compares universal features of

1

human language with characteristics of other primate communication systems, on the assumption that our closest primate "cousins" can in some way represent the primate ancestral group that we have in common with them. A third approach equates stages of linguistic development in children with stages of linguistic evolution. All three approaches are capable of generating interesting and useful speculations as well as improbable, even ridiculous, hypotheses. The difference between useful and ridiculous in this context lies in the skill with which the data are generated, integrated, and interpreted. Such skill depends in turn on an understanding of what language is, how it operates in human society, and how it articulates with the rest of culture.

LANGUAGE AS CODE

We all have some notion of what language is. My nine-year-old nephew defines language as "words and the ways that we string them together and pronounce them to communicate ideas." Not bad, for this embodies in simplified terms the technical categories "lexicon," "syntax," "phonology," and "semantics." But then, like so many definitions, it really doesn't tell us much by itself. Let's begin instead with a slightly more precise characterization of language—one that can be dissected a bit more easily:

Fewer than one hundred sounds which are individually meaningless are compounded, not in all possible ways, to produce some hundreds of thousands of meaningful morphemes which have meanings that are arbitrarily assigned, and these morphemes are combined by rule to yield an infinite set of sentences, having meanings that can be derived.[1]

With this kind of communication system we are able to transmit emotionally neutral messages that have never been sent before; messages that can be correctly understood by anyone using the same code; messages referring to things remote in space and time; messages that can be quite complicated, yet readily understood even in the absence of face-to-face interaction. A communication system with these capabilities sets us apart from all other animals. It enables us to develop writing, mathematics, telephones, airplanes, radios, and atomic bombs to name but a few cultural artifacts that would never exist but for language.

We bring many cognitive skills to the task of learning a language, as well as the motivation to learn it. These skills are inborn in the sense that they unfold in a genetically controlled sequence. Only extreme physical handicaps can prevent a human child from learning to speak; yet no other animal has ever mastered a human language, although recent experiments with chimpanzees demonstrate some remarkably languagelike capabilities (see chapter 5). What we don't bring to the task of language acquisition is an innate knowledge of sound discriminations that must be made, of permissible sound sequences, of word forms and the meanings associated with them, and of the ways in which words must be combined to convey intended messages. These things are specific to the language being acquired and must be learned. In learning a language, the child uses his wired-in but constantly developing cognitive skills to perceive and extract regularities from the welter of linguistic input to which he is exposed. Eventually he will have internalized a linguistic system quite like that of his parents.

An individual's internalized linguistic system, the knowledge enabling him to produce and understand an infinite number of sentences, is his linguistic *competence*. This linguistic competence is sometimes called a

---

1. Roger Brown, *Social Psychology* (New York: The Free Press, 1965), p. 248.

competence grammar. The sentences that he actually produces, whether grammatical or not, constitute his linguistic *performance*.[2] Competence is not available for direct observation. It must be inferred from performance.

The distinction between competence and performance is similar to that which separates language from speech. *Language* is the system itself, a system of inferred rules upon which behavior is based. *Speech* is the vocal manifestation or application of this linguistic system. Since it is difficult to imagine speech apart from social contexts in which it occurs, we will ultimately have to deal directly with the interaction situation, with speech in its natural habitat. But let's not open the door to that just yet.

To simplify exposition, we shall continue the convenient fiction that language is a referential system only: that it provides the linkage between the sounds that we hear and the objects, events, qualities, and ideas to which the sound sequences refer. It would be oversimplification, however, to suggest that the linkage between sound and referent is direct or uncomplicated. To the contrary, the relationship is indirect and complex, going from a very concrete level of organization—sound manifestations—to a highly abstract level—concepts. The abstract conceptual level is linked in turn to the concrete world of objects and events by a complex process known as perception. Think of the words "justice," "yesterday," "unicorn," "Horatio," "ache," or "Jupiter," and it becomes apparent that referential meaning is really represented as concepts, configurations, or entities in the mind, rather than out there in nature.

PHONOLOGY

Speech originates in the brain. A complex network of nerves leads from an area in the dominant hemisphere to control operations of the tongue and other articulators, the size and shape of the vocal tract, and the vocal cords. When you breathe or talk, air passes through the glottal opening between vocal cords as well as through your throat (*pharyngeal cavity*) and mouth (*oral cavity*) or nose (*nasal cavity*). Speech sounds come about through modifications of the breath stream on its journey through these areas.

When the vocal cords close your glottis, creating vibrations, the vowels and consonants of speech are said to be *voiced*. You can feel this by touching your Adam's apple. An open glottis, on the other hand, produces *voiceless* sounds (e.g., *p, t, k, s, f*). The vocal cords, varying in length and shape from one person to another, produce a fundamental tone quality which can be varied as in singing and which together with characteristics of a person's vocal chambers (e.g., size of nasal cavity) determine the distinctive background voice qualities setting off one person's speech from everyone else's. Women usually have shorter vocal cords than men, so their tonal range is about an octave higher.

A guitar string played in open air gives a very thin sound. The sound is made fuller when it resonates through the large chamber of the guitar's body. Our three resonance chambers, the pharynx, mouth, and nose, add secondary vibrations to the basic sounds emitted by vibrating vocal cords. What comes out are the sounds of speech.

Size and shape of the oral cavity in particular can be varied tremendously. It can not only be narrowed and elongated, it can also be closed or partially closed by actions of the tongue and lips. Complete momentary closure of the mouth or pharyngeal

2. For a more detailed and broadened discussion of the competence-performance distinction see Dell Hymes, "Competence and Performance in Linguistic Theory," in *Language Acquisition: Models and Methods,* eds. R. Huxley and E. Ingram (New York: Academic Press, 1971), pp. 3-23.

cavities at any given place produces a class of sounds known as *stops* which can be either voiced (*b, d, g*) or voiceless (*p, t, k, ʔ*). If closure is not quite complete, the friction produces another class of sounds known as *fricatives* (*f, s, v, z*). A stop and fricative produced together in rapid sequence results in an *affricate* (e.g., *č*—conventional notation for the *ch* in "child," *ǰ*—the *j* in "jack"). Stops, fricatives, and affricates represent different *manners of articulation,* but they are all *obstruents,* consonants that cannot function as syllable nuclei—the usual function of vowels.

Sounds that are not obstruents can be called *sonorants.* Sonorants carry the melody and accent in speech. This category of

sounds can be subdivided into the *vowels* (*a, e, i, o, u*), *semivowels* (*w, y*), *liquids* (*l, r*), and *nasals* (*m, n, ŋ*).

Consonants and semivowels can be classified by place of articulation in addition to manner and voicing. *Labials* include *p, b, f,* and *w* as well as several sounds unfamiliar to English speakers. *Dentals* include *t, d, s,* and *z* among others. *Palatals* include *č, ǰ, š, ž,* and *y. Velars* include *k, g,* and *ŋ. Uvular* sounds, rarely heard in America, are important in several languages including French and Kekchi. *Glottals* include the voiceless stop *ʔ* and the voiceless fricative *h.* Using the dimensions of voicing, manner of articulation, and point of articulation we can readily identify any consonant, as when we say that *b* is a voiced bilabial stop. Vowels are easier to deal with in terms of the dimensions tongue height and frontness-backness, as can be seen in the phonetic chart.

In addition to the above sound segments, there are *suprasegmental* qualities such as pitch and stress which are superimposed on syllable nuclei during speech. These can have language specific referential importance as when we use stress to differentiate "pérvert" (the noun) from "pervért" (the verb), or they can be primarily expressive in function.

We hear utterances that are really quite continuous, but we manage to divide them into discrete segments with relative ease. The elementary sound segments of a particular language are its *phonemes,* roughly corresponding to the letters with which we spell words. The word "pit," for example, can be analyzed into three distinct sound units, *p, i,* and *t.* We know that *p* and *b* represent two different phonemes in English because substituting *b* for the *p* in "pit" results in a word "bit" that has a different meaning. The phonemes *p* and *b* are meaningful units in English even though neither one can be assigned any particular meaning by itself. In some languages the sounds that

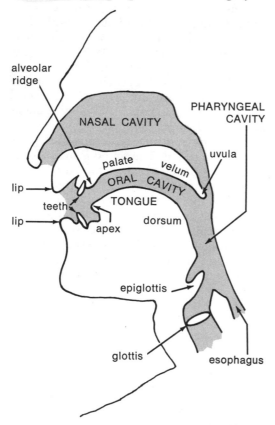

Figure 1.1 THE SPEECH ORGANS

we represent as *p* and *b* are simply different manifestations of a single phoneme. Substituting one for the other will not change the referential meaning of a word in which either appears.

Although we may feel that the *p* sound in "pit" is pronounced the same as the *p* sound in "spit," they are actually quite different. If you hold your hand a few inches in front of your mouth you can feel a puff of air, called *aspiration,* when you articulate the *p* in "pit." No such feeling attends the *p* in "spit," nor will you hear any aspiration. Clearly the single English phoneme /*p*/ (written inside slashes to signal its phonemic status) has two different phonetic manifestations in the words "pit" and "spit." All variant pronunciations of the same essential sound, or phoneme, in a particular language are called *allophones* of the phoneme. Some variants have predictable—and complementary or mutually exclusive—distributions as in the example given, for in English *p, t,* and *k* (voiceless stops) are normally aspirated if they begin a word. If, on the other hand, they follow an *s* in the same syllable, none of these stops will be aspirated. Such variation in the pronunciation of a phoneme is called *conditioned variation:* variation determined by some aspect of the environment in which an abstract entity—here a phoneme—is manifested.

	labial		dental		velar	uvular	glottal
STOPS voiceless	p		t		k	q	ʔ
voiced	b		d		g	ɢ	
FRICATIVES Slit, vl.	ɸ	f	θ		x	h	
Slit, vd	β	v	ð		γ		
Groove vl.			s š				
Groove vd.			z ž				
Lateral, vl			ɫ				
AFFRICATES Groove, vl.			ƛ č				
Groove, vd.			ǰ				
RESONANTS Nasal	m		n	ñ	ŋ		
Lateral			l				
Median	w		r	y			

		Front	Central	Back
High		i	ɨ	u
Lower High		ɪ		ʊ
Mid		e	ə	o
Lower Mid		E		ɔ
Low		æ	a	

Figure 1.2 PHONETIC CHART

Variation for which conditioning environments are not specified, variation that cannot be predicted by rules, is *free variation*.

A moment's reflection may lead one to reject the above example of predictable distribution by imagining a situation in which "spit" could easily be articulated with an aspirated *p*, such as when the speaker is angry. Distribution is still predictable, but environmental conditioning must be more strictly specified to include expressive functions of speech in this case. In English aspiration is subphonemic—it doesn't distinguish one phoneme from another. That is why we can use it expressively (e.g., to express anger) by including it where it would not normally occur. This subject, departing from referential meaning, will be introduced again in the present chapter.

Phonemes, then, can be regarded as classes of related sounds that speakers of a particular language regard as a single sound. We have seen that aspirated *p* [*p*ʰ] and unaspirated *p* are treated by English speakers as the same sound. A Bolivian speaker of Quechua, however, would hear them as different sounds belonging to two different phonemes. Two words, identical except that one has an aspirated *p* and the other an unaspirated *p*, will mean different things in Quechua. Every language divides up the universe of possible sounds differently: each possesses its own uniquely constituted set of phonemes.

While English makes use of thirty-three segmental phonemes, some languages have as few as twelve and others have as many as sixty. Because the phonemes of a language are patterned in a way that is unique to the individual language, and because these abstract units are related by rules to the actual sounds that we hear in ways that are language specific, we cannot directly compare phonemes across languages. This is a formidable problem if we want to make phonological generalizations about language.

The task of interlanguage sound system comparison can be accomplished, however, by decomposing phoneme segments not into classes of alternative sounds, but into bundles of simultaneous signalling units, or *features*, such as nasality, voicing, glottalization, and so on. Thus the phoneme /p/ in "pit" can be described as a combination of the three features labial, stop, and voiceless. These features alone are enough to distinguish it from any other English phoneme beginning a word, and can be called, therefore, the *distinctive features* of /p/. Although the *p* in "pit" is aspirated, the feature aspiration is a predictable manifestation of /p/ in this context and therefore nondistinctive: it is a redundant feature that is not needed to specify this phoneme.[3] Feature constituents of phonemes, rather than phonemes themselves, can be compared across languages.

By carefully selecting appropriate articulatory, auditory, and acoustic properties, it is possible to specify a pool of about fifteen features from which every language draws for its phonemic distinctions. A feature approach to interlanguage comparisons makes a great deal of sense. As we have seen, it would be meaningless to ask how many languages have the /p/ phoneme. It is possible, on the other hand, to ask how many languages utilize a particular feature (e.g., voicing) to create phonemic oppositions (e.g., between *p* and *b*), and how any given language might pattern its use of a particular feature. This is important and will be brought up again in chapter 6.

Earlier I mentioned that some features are distinctive and some are redundant. This redundancy is an important part of language. Redundant features help us to identify the

---

3. To characterize the *p* in "spit" we need only specify the features labial and stop. Since voiced labial stops never occur after an *s* in English, to include the feature voiceless here would be redundant.

words that we hear because background noise and other sorts of communicative interference make necessary many secondary clues to help the listener in message interpretation. Redundancy in human language, in fact, remains right around the 50 percent level.

Another source of redundancy, apart from feature redundancy, derives from the fact that while our words are formed from combinations of phonemes, not every hypothetically possible phoneme sequence actually occurs in any language. In English, for example, no word will begin with a /bd/ or /ŋ/, nor does any word end with an /h/. Limitations on permissible sound sequences in a language can be described by general rules, rules predicting redundant characteristics in the physical manifestation of speech forms. Predictable characteristics constitute one kind of redundancy. Repetition, as when we repeat a word for someone who didn't hear it the first time, is another kind of redundancy.

MORPHOLOGY

Words are the lifeblood of language, making the transition from sound to meaning possible. Each word can be thought of as representing a particular group of phonological and semantic properties—properties that are exchanged when we encode (speak) or decode (hear) linguistic messages. Each word also has syntactic properties. That is, it can combine with other words to form sentences, but only in rather restricted ways. For example, "sky" is a noun which can be combined with "blue," "the," and "is" in only two possible ways to result in a well-formed sentence: "The sky is blue" or "Is the sky blue?" Other permutations, such as "Sky the is blue," ignore the syntactic properties of these words.

Words participate in larger grammatical units like the phrase, clause, and sentence. They also can be broken down into smaller units carrying referential meaning, minimal units of this type being called *morphemes*. The word "cats," for example, consists of two morphemes, {cat} and the plural morpheme commonly represented as {Z}. These morphemes have a fixed order with respect to one another. To put it another way, words are internally stable combinations of morphemes.

Morphology is that aspect of grammatical description which deals with the internal structure of words, or—more narrowly—with rules by which morphemes are combined to form words. At first sight it may seem uncomplicated to formulate such rules. Couldn't we, for example, deal with nouns in English by saying that the plural morpheme is simply added to the end of the singular form as in "cats?" In most cases this rule with some further phonological specifications will work: but what about "deer," or "feet"? The former remains the same whether singular or plural, and the latter adds no plural marker to the end of the singular form, but depends instead on a vowel substitution to differentiate singular and plural. Static rules of arrangement are not sufficient, then, to relate the semantic properties of words to their phonological properties. It is necessary in some cases—while merely useful in others—to have rules of process which operate on some basic or underlying form, changing it to another in the appropriate contexts. Thus the underlying representation {foot} is manifested as "foot" when singular and as "feet" when plural, "foot" becoming "feet" by vowel change.

Linguists commonly distinguish *free morphemes*, forms that can stand alone as words (e.g., "cat," "go," "red,"), from *bound morphemes* which have to be attached to other morphemes (e.g., "-ness," "-ing," "un-," or the plural morpheme {Z}. This division corresponds closely to the distinction between *roots* and *affixes*, roots being the basic forms which are modified by the addition of affixes to them. The roots of a language greatly outnumber the affixes, a useful point to remember.

Words, sometimes called *lexemes,* may be single free morphemes (e.g., "cat"), *compounds* of two or more free morphemes (e.g., "doghouse"), or free morphemes combined with one or more bound morphemes (e.g., "farmers"). Bound morphemes are affixed (prefixed, infixed, or suffixed) to the rest of a word. Some bound morphemes simply change words from one part of speech to another, as when "-ness" is suffixed to the adjective "sad" resulting in a noun "sadness." Others, such as the plural morpheme or the past tense morpheme, do not change the part of speech of the words involved. These two kinds of morphemes signal different types of information, the former typifying *derivational* affixes and the latter characteristic of *inflectional* affixes which usually are attached only after the root has been modified already by any derivational affixes that it needs.

Some morphemes have several different phonological manifestations, called *allomorphs,* which may be determined by phonetic properties of surrounding morphemes. Let's recall the plural morpheme { Z } as an illustration. It is a bound morpheme that changes its shape to conform to phonetic properties of the words to which it is attached. Phonemically these variant shapes of { Z } are /-s/ (when added to such words as "cat," "lock," or "top"), /-ɨz/ (when added to such words as "church," "glass," or "bush"), and /-z/ (when added to such words as "dog," "car," or "pan"). If you listen closely to your own pronunciation of these words, you will see that there really are three different ways of pronouncing the same plural that we write with an ⁻s. It is the sound directly preceding the plural ending that determines which of the three allomorphs will occur. In rule form, we could say that { Z } is manifested as /ɨz/ after /s,

z, š, ž, č, and ǰ/, as /s/ after any other obstruent if it is voiceless, and as /z/ after any other voiced sound. As English speakers we follow this rule quite unconsciously, applying it even to nonsense words made up on the spur-of-the-moment. Rules of this sort, determining the phonemic shapes of morphemes on the basis of phonetic conditioning environments, are often termed *morphophonemic* rules.

There is another way of describing the formation of plurals in English (apart from the few exceptions like "oxen," "sheep," "mice," etc., which must be listed and learned separately). We can propose that the underlying phonemic representation of the plural is /-z/ which is acted on by two more general rules of English phonology to specify correct surface representations whenever the rules are applicable. The first rule roughly stated specifies that an /ɨ/ must be inserted between any two obstruents sharing basically the same point and manner of articulation. From this rule we get /kisɨz/ "kisses" from underlying /kisz/, for example. The second rule, which applies only after /i/ insertion, specifies that all consonants in a consonant cluster must be voiceless if the first one is voiceless. From this second rule we get /lips/ "lips" from underlying /lipz/, for example. These two rules apply quite generally in the sound system of English and help to account for the various manifestations of possessive and past tense inflection as well as plurals. The simplicity and productivity of this process-oriented approach is appealing, and it is beginning to replace the older arrangement-oriented approach illustrated just above it.

Languages differ in the means by which they express such concepts as plurality, negation, interrogation, tense, mood, shape, comparison, and so on. Of all the possible ways that a concept *could* be expressed, each language chooses some and ignores others. Moreover, several different means may be employed within a single language to express any given concept. As we have seen, plural formation in English takes place primarily in the morphological system through addition of a single bound morpheme suffix, although a few words are pluralized with different suffixes ("ox": "oxen"), internal vowel changes ("man": "men"), or no change at all ("deer": "deer"). Other existing languages express plurality with prefixes, infixes, tone changes, or separate free morphemes.

The fact that all known languages have some means for expressing plurality even though the means may differ substantially illustrates an important principle: that superficial differences often belie underlying similarities. The converse of this, that superficial similarities among languages often belie differences that become apparent only on closer inspection, is another point to remember. Tzeltal, an Indian language of Mexico, for example, seems to express plurality very much like English. For most nouns there is a single plural suffix / – etik/. A closer look, however, indicates that the "singular" (uninflected for plural) form of the noun actually means either singular or plural, depending on context, so that plural suffixes are frequently omitted even when the noun has a plural referent. In fact, the plural suffix is never used on nouns when preceded by numbers: *ča-tul ʔač'iš*, literally "two-person girl" means "two girls," for example. English speakers have to mark plural in count nouns referring to more than one thing, even when this is redundant as in "two girls." Tzeltal speakers shave off some of this redundancy because Tzeltal has *facultative* expression of the plural; they have a plural marker (a suffix), but they don't have to use it to convey the notion of plurality.

SYNTAX

Morphology is concerned with the internal structure of words, syntax with the internal structure of sentences. Both levels of organization involve the sequential arrangement of morphemes, so syntax can be construed to include morphology; and modern usage of the term syntax does just that. When we are dealing with a language such as English, in which a distinction between words and sentences can be made fairly easily, it may be useful to distinguish morphology from syntax. In other languages like Eskimo, where words very often are complete and complex sentences, the distinction is less useful.

To construct a sentence in any language we need to do two fundamental things, representing the syntactic processes *selection* and *arrangement*. First we must choose the words that best convey our thoughts. Then we have to arrange them in an appropriate order with the proper modifications—additions, deletions, and substitutions—so that they will conform to grammatical restrictions on sentence construction dictated by the language. To illustrate this point let's imagine that we witnessed a particularly surly canine biting the postman and wanted to tell someone about it without giving any more information about the event than absolutely necessary, so we have selected only the words "bite," "dog," and "man." The job just can't be done in acceptable English with only these three words.

It would be ungrammatical to say "bite dog man" even though these alone are the vocabulary items originally selected to convey the intended message—translations of just these words in just this order would form a grammatical and appropriate sentence in many languages, but not English. A bit more sense can be made of the words when we arrange them as "dog bite man," but this is still not enough. The rules of English grammar force us to specify both nouns "dog" and "man" and to mark the verb "bite" for tense. Of several alternative possibilities, one solution would result in the grammatical and appropriate sentence "A dog bit the man." *Word order* here signals the grammatical relationships of subject and direct object (actor and acted-upon) as can be readily seen if we reverse the order of noun phrases with respect to the verb (i.e., "The man bit a dog"). Furthermore we have marked "dog" with the indefinite article by preceding it with "a," marked "man" with a preceding "the," and inflected "bite" for past tense in conformity with morphological rules of English. The point here is that syntactic rules of a language, like morphological ones, provide strong limitations on the spoken manifestations of messages we want to express.

Syntactic rules also give us tremendous power to create new, different, and complicated spoken messages. *Substitution* of entities within a sentence frame is one syntactic device which can function either to cut out needless repetition or to amplify the information content of any portion of the sentence. If, for example, the postman who was bitten above is already the subject of conversation between speaker and hearer, we can substitute the pronoun "him" for the noun phrase "the man," yielding "A dog bit him." Or, if we want to give more information about the dog involved, we might substitute "the big spotted dog that lives up the street" for "a dog," yielding "the big spotted dog that lives up the street bit the man." Note here that when we substituted "him" for "the man," the pronoun "he" took the form "him" in accordance with an English syntactic rule reflecting remnants of an older and more pervasive case system; and that the clause "that lives up the street" embedded in the second sentence is *subordinated* to "the big spotted dog," and is functioning here as an adjectival modifier of the noun phrase preceding it.

Subordination is actually a relationship holding between sentence constituents on many different levels. In the sentence, "I know that the postman likes small dogs," "small" is subordinated to "dogs" just as

the subordinate clause "that the postman likes small dogs" is subordinated to the main clause "I know." Look again and you will see a whole sentence embedded in the subordinate clause, which shows how complex sentences can be derived by applying syntactic rules to combinations of simpler sentences.

Like rules for subordination, syntactic rules of *coordination* allow us to join two or more sentences together in several different ways. We could use the conjunction "and," for example, to put "John went to school" next to "Mary went to the store," forming the single sentence "John went to school and Mary went to the store." A *deletion* rule, one kind of substitution, could be applied here to cut out the repeated verb, which would give us "John went to school and Mary to the store." These two sentences differ slightly in their make-up, but they give essentially the same information and hence are *paraphrases* of one another.

Linguists (usually) judiciously use paraphrases to identify and characterize rules of sentence transformation—rules of deletion, insertion, and rearrangement—which are applied to sentence constituents in the process of changing an original sentence or combination of several sentences into the several possible paraphrases that can be derived. As we saw for process-oriented phonology and morphology, this involves postulating an underlying representation of abstract entities along with rules—some of them applying in a specific order with respect to one another—for arriving at the various possible surface representations which are paraphrases of each other. Many linguists today feel that transformational rules not only derive different paraphrases from the same underlying conceptual representation, but they introduce all of the morphological and syntactic trappings necessary to convert underlying conceptual representations into surface sentence manifestations. Among other things, rules of insertion, deletion, and rearrangement operate at various points in the derivation of a sentence to create words, to inflect for tense, number, and so on, to insert such dummy items as "it" in "It is raining," to make a sentence or smaller constituent negative, to change a statement into a question or a command, and to make an active sentence passive.

Two further syntactic processes should be mentioned here, special kinds of *co-occurrence restrictions*. They are *concord* (or agreement) and *government*. These forbidding words refer to quite simple processes involving the modification of words to conform to demands of other words co-occurring in the same sentence. Concord is merely a mutual dependency in form among words in a sentence. For example, "that" must be changed to "those" if it is qualifying a plural noun, as in "those men" or "those dogs"; if one stem requires the plural inflection, both do. Government is when the form of one word is determined by some syntactic characteristic of another, as in "the dog bit him" rather than "the dog bit he." English makes very little use of concord and government; other languages, like Latin, a great deal.

All languages convey information about things, events, and qualities, so it is not surprising that all have sentences in which we can isolate nounlike forms (nominals), verblike forms (verbals), adjectivelike forms (adjectivals), and adverblike forms (adverbials). Words belonging to these four classes are called *content words*. They convey more information than those belonging to other word classes. The other word classes, such as conjunctions, prepositions, determiners, and auxiliaries, give less information and often function primarily or exclusively to mark and specify relations among content words. These are called *function words*. Languages with few function words depend to a greater extent on affixes or root modification to signal these

relations than do those with many. Function words are important syntactic devices, then, some of which also carry semantic information. They are part of the glue which holds together the meanings of sentences.

Because you speak a language, you are capable of making up an infinite number of different sentences that can be readily understood by anyone speaking your language, even if the sentences have never been uttered. And you can do this with a vocabulary that may comprise no more than a few thousand morphemes. An incredible feat? Certainly, but all humans are capable of performing it. Rules for selection, substitution, arrangement, coordination, and subordination of sentence constituents—syntactic rules—make this possible.

Whereas morphemes, words, and idiomatic expressions have "dictionary meanings," syntactic rules contribute another sort of meaning to utterances which we can call "grammatical meaning," conveying such information as which sentence constituent is the indirect object or the subject, or which noun is being modified by an adjective. To put it another way, concepts and their interrelationships are expressed in sentences through operation of a linguistic code which allows us to attribute referential meaning to them. Language viewed as a referential system is responsible for communicating only a fraction of the total information that gets communicated when we speak.

PARALANGUAGE

Other communicative systems are superimposed on the linguistic one, augmenting or modifying the messages communicated by language in speech. One such system, overlapping the linguistic system, can be called *paralanguage*. Paralanguage includes all of the sounds coming from your mouth and nose that are not directly part of language. For the most part they accompany speech (e.g., drawling, whispering, shouting), but they can also convey messages in place of speech (e.g., shushing, wolf whistling, hissing). We can conveniently distinguish three separate subgroupings under the broad heading paralanguage. First there is the *voice set,* the physically and physiologically determined characteristics of an individual's voice that serve as a background for evaluating meaningful paralinguistic variations. One's voice set identifies him as a particular individual, and can give the listener information about his sex, health, age, body build, and even location.

Against a background of voice set, the listener measures two other aspects of paralanguage: vocal segregates and voice qualities. *Vocal segregates* include the many vocalizations we make that are expressive but not really a part of language. We can say *brrr* to indicate that it is cold, grunt "yes" or "no," make several varieties of tongue clicking for approval or disapproval, imitate a cock crowing, shush a noisy child, or hiss at a bad movie. These are all vocal segregates, and they can convey some rather specific messages.

Voice qualities include the loudness, pitch, and length variations superimposed on syllable nuclei that in some languages make referential distinctions. If they are distinctive referentially, then they are part of the linguistic system. Where they do not play a part in the linguistic system, they are free to signal paralinguistic information. Other voice qualities that can accompany speech are whining, yawning, moaning, whispering, whimpering, giggling, laughing, and crying, as well as qualities interlocking these—tempo (from fast to slow), rhythm (from smooth to jerky), resonance (from thin to full-bodied), and others. Voice qualities can tell the listener if we are nervous, confident, angry, exuberant, irritated, or calm. That is, they are indicators of our emotional state among other things. Such information, naturally, is very important for the interpretation of vocal messages.

GESTURE

The man before you is very nervous. The side of his face is twitching. He keeps crossing and uncrossing his legs during the interview. His hands move jerkily as he points to a passage in the book. You note that he swallows and blinks frequently, and that his face is flushed. All are stereotypical signs of nervousness and are all conveyed through *gesture.* If we define the domain of gesture to include all visible body activity, we can divide it up in a way that neatly parallels paralanguage. First we must identify *gesture set* as the physical and physiological peculiarities of an individual's visible body activity which serve as a background for evaluating meaningful gestural variations. Like voice set, gesture set can give information about an individual's age, sex, health, and sanity.

Against a background of gesture set can be measured *gesture qualities* such as speed (from fast to slow), flow (from smooth to jerky), degree (from barely noticeable to pronounced), and others. These qualities can apply equally well to activities of the face, limbs, and posture. *Gestural segregates* such as a nod or shake of the head, a pointing finger, a good-bye wave of the hand, crossed legs, finger snapping, slapping the thigh, clapping, or a friendly wink have varying degrees of culturally determined meaning. They can be executed and described with reference to the gesture qualities noted above. Above all, they convey information that can amplify, emphasize, or modify linguistic and paralinguistic messages as well as information which can be transmitted in the absence of any vocal communication. As with the vocal-auditory mode of communication, the gestural-visual mode is always manifested in a social context, and it is the total context which provides the means necessary for interpretation of any message.

Gestural communication, often called *kinesics,* also has its analogue to language. That is, in some societies or social groupings within societies communication takes place through a gesture language. American sign language, for example, is a language for the deaf. It utilizes a vocabulary of gestural signs which combine in rule-governed ways to form gestural sentences. Possessing a vocabulary and syntax, a gesture language can be considered coordinate with, rather than necessarily subordinate to, a language proper. It performs similar functions, slightly differently expressed.

In addition to the vocal-auditory and visual-gestural channels of communication, we also transmit some information that is perceived through the senses of smell, taste, and touch. Most obvious are such things as kissing, spanking, wearing perfume, shaking hands, and hugging. You can probably

I   Vocal-Auditory (Hearing)

   A   Voice Set

   B   Voice Qualities

   C   Vocal Segregates

   D   Language

II   Gestural-Visual (Sight)

   A   Gesture Set

   B   Gesture Qualities

   C   Gestural Qualities

   D   Gesture Language

III   Touch

IV   Taste

V   Smell

Figure 1.3   MODES OF COMMUNICATION

think of many more to add to these. One day, perhaps, these communicative modes will be studied as closely as vocal and gestural communication have been.

SEMANTICS

In a nutshell, semantics is the study of meaning. The nature of meaning and the way that it should be represented in a linguistic model, or grammar, is the most crucial and disputed question in current linguistic theory. Up to this point I have taken pains to restrict linguistic meaning to referential meaning only. At this level the "I'm hungry" uttered by a starving beggar has the same meaning as the "I'm hungry" said by a child to his mother at bedtime when he wants to stay up a little longer.[4] The linguist has until recently been content to treat these utterances as identical with respect to meaning, and has referred to the sort of meaning shared by them as "core meaning," "literal meaning," "dictionary meaning," "primary meaning," or "referential meaning." Linguistic models predicated on this kind of meaning disregard the fact that these two utterances may differ in voice qualities of the speakers, desired goals of the speakers, intonational patterns of the speakers, gestural accompaniments to the utterances, cultural knowledge and presumptions of the speakers and hearers, inferences made by the hearers, and appropriateness of the utterances in context among other things. In short they must disregard vast quantities of information transmitted by the two speech acts which are not common to both.

On the other side of the coin, we can think of situations in which "Shut the door," "It's noisy in here," "Would you be so kind," or simply a pointed finger could all be con-

4. Leonard Bloomfield, *Language* (New York: Holt, Rinehart and Winston, 1933), pp. 141-42.

sidered functionally equivalent requests, sharing the same pragmatic meaning. Again, linguistic models of the sort mentioned above have to treat each of them differently, ignoring the level of meaning that they share.

As meaning has become a focal question for linguistics in the last few years, some theoretical linguists have come to see language as a system that cannot be clearly analyzed apart from other cultural systems of communication, apart from the social contexts in which it is manifested, apart from the social meanings that figure prominantly in determining some aspects of sentence structure. These linguists have found it necessary in making judgments of grammaticality and in defining constraints on co-occurrence of sentence constituents to augment the core referential meaning traditionally associated with linguistic form by considering other meaningful characteristics of utterances. Utterances, or sentences, are then seen to encode not only core meanings but also *entailed propositions* (e.g., "John's baldness caused him much worry" entails the proposition "John was bald"), *presupposed propositions* (e.g., "Mary was bald" must be interpreted in the light of such presuppositions as that "Mary probably hides it with a wig," "Women are more rarely bald than men," and "Mary is probably a woman because Mary is a woman's name"), *implied propositions* (e.g., "John wasn't really happy until yesterday" can imply that "John has been really happy since yesterday"), and *illocutionary propositions* (e.g., "Shut the door" includes the unstated illocutionary proposition "I am commanding you" as a necessary part of the sentence).

Language as a system, abstracted from social situations, limited to neutral or normal referential meanings of utterances, and restricted to inferred grammatical rules pertaining to an idealized speaker-hearer in a homogeneous speech community, is a legitimate concern of structural linguistics. Some-

where along the way, however, speech in context inclusive of variation slipped in the back door of linguistic study and has become the central concern of sociolinguistics.

SOCIOLINGUISTICS

Language seen in terms of a single referential function has for many years been a useful way to separate and intensively study a communicative system that can be to some extent distinguished analytically from other systems of human communication with which it articulates. The fact is, however, that language is typically manifested in situated speech events, in social contexts within which it is often difficult to distinguish linguistic elements from nonlinguistic ones. Many communicative functions are manifested in the same speech act; many kinds of information are conveyed from one person to another. Hence the spoken utterance in context weaves social and grammatical knowledge together, often inseparably so.

Looking at it another way, the child who is acquiring language is simultaneously learning his society's rules for when to speak and when not to; when to use respect forms, baby talk, slang, or a secret language; how to open and close conversations; how to announce, apologize, congratulate, or explain in a culturally approved manner; when to quote, and numerous other commuicative skills—sociolinguistic skills that so clearly go hand in hand with the acquisition of language. A child who grew up capable of generating grammatically correct utterances but who couldn't create and choose appropriate ones at the right time would certainly be a monster.

Each of us, then, has our own repertoire of sociolinguistic knowledge that we draw upon for better or for worse to say what we have to say. And what we have to say is interpreted or misinterpreted on the basis of our listener's repertoire of sociolinguistic knowledge. To the extent that individual repertoires have shared features or can be made to mesh through continuing establishment of common understandings, communication is effective.

Effective communication within a social group underlies the basic sociolinguistic concept of *speech community,* "a community sharing knowledge of rules for the conduct and interpretation of speech."[5] Within a speech community one can isolate many situations in which specifiable rules governing the use of speech characterize particular *speech events.* A speech event can be composed of one or more *speech acts,* these being minimal communicative acts employing verbal means, which can occur in one or more situational contexts. Dell Hymes, an American pioneer in the field of sociolinguistics who is responsible for these terms, notes as illustration that in our society a joke can occur in such varied contexts as a lecture, a formal introduction, or a sermon; "joke" is the label that we give to this speech act. A joke (speech act) may also occur within a conversation (speech event) that takes place during a party (speech situation). Every society has its own criteria for defining and naming speech acts, speech events, and speech situations; and every society has its own values with respect to the importance of various components and functions of speech acts.

A speech act can be dissected in terms of seven essential components: (1) sender; (2) receiver; (3) message form; (4) message channel; (5) topic; (6) code; (7) setting.[6] Nine broad functions, any of which may or may not be emphasized in any particular speech act, are potentially applicable to the speech act as a whole. Each function can be attributed to a primary association with one of the seven speech act components.

The *sender* (or speaker) need not always be a human. There are societies in which a musical instrument, certain animals, or even a clap of thunder may be the sender in a speech act. Sounds produced by the sender can function to tell the receiver something about the speaker's age, sex, area of origin, and often other personal features; his voice set, intonation, rhythm, speed, pronunciation, vocabulary, and style serve, in short, to identify him. This is the *identification function.*

Choice of words, intonation, relative speed of response, and other aspects of the speaker's vocal performance may also function expressively, to express emotions and attitudes towards the receiver or any other component of the speech act. The *expressive function* is particularly apparent when it operates in opposition to the referential meaning of what has been said. Consider, for example, the child who tries to avoid a scolding by saying, "I only said that you're a real nice person, Mommy." But her mother isn't fooled and replies, "It's not the words (referential function) that bother me, but the way (expressive function) that you said them."

Potential *channels* of communication in various societies include gestures, whistling, and drumming, as well as speech. Principally associated with message channel is the *contact function,* whether physical in the sense of sound waves hitting the receiver's ear, or psychological in the sense of speaking just to be speaking. Communication for its own sake is an important part of social life and is found more highly developed in some people than in others. Perhaps you

5. Dell Hymes, *Foundations in Sociolinguistics* (Philadelphia: University of Pennsylvania Press, 1974), p. 51. Subsequent definitions of sociolinguistic concepts are also adapted from Hymes.

6. These components are set forth with more illustrative detail in Dell Hymes, "The Ethnography of Speaking," in *Anthropology and Human Behavior,* eds. T. Gladwin and W. C. Sturtevant (Washington, D. C.: Anthropological Society of Washington, 1962), pp. 13-53. They have been modified and augmented by several additional speech act components in subsequent articles by Hymes.

have noticed that often in elevators people speak simply to maintain psychological contact. Silence in our own culture, when prolonged, could in some circumstances be interpreted as implied hostility. Pleasant but noninformative verbal rituals, as on meeting a friend or talking to a stranger in an elevator, serve to allay anxiety; the receiver thereby learns something of the sender's intentions.

The *form* of a message can be said to have a *poetic function*. Though not limited to poetry, the poetic function is expressed as restrictions on message form. There are different degrees and varieties of aesthetic pleasure derivable from various ways of formulating a message with any given referential content.

The *referential function* in speech is most directly associated with the *topic* of a speech act, and is closely tied to the "dictionary meanings" of messages. When we take something literally, we are appealing to the referential function, which is the key function for structural description of language.

The *code* component of a speech act refers to the signalling units of which messages are composed and to the rules for combining these units. When we speak of phonemes, morphemes, and sentences, we refer to elements of the linguistic code. Similarly we can think of technical jargon, slang, formal speech, and other levels and varieties of speech, as well as dialects and languages, as codes or combinations of several codes. The *metalinguistic function* is associated primarily with the code(s) involved. Information about the code which is conveyed in a speech act is metalinguistic information. We consciously manifest an interest in the metalinguistic function when we ask questions like "What language is that?" "How do you spell it?" or "Are you sure that's not just slang?"

When we focus attention on the *receiver* in a speech act, two general functions can be involved: one directive and the other

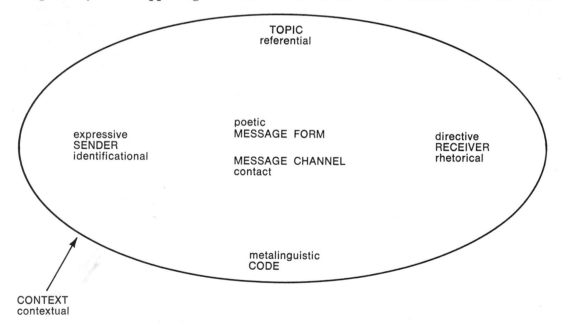

Figure 1.4 COMPONENTS AND FUNCTIONS OF THE SPEECH ACT

rhetorical. The *directive function* concerns subsequent activity of the receiver as directed by what the speaker says. The *rhetorical function* concerns the receiver's outlook as it is affected by what is said. These two functions correspond to overt behavior on the one hand and to attitudes and beliefs on the other. They are interrelated in that subsequent activity is partly determined by attitude or outlook.

The *setting* component is defined in terms of criteria that may involve all six of the other components. Relevant features which constitute a particular setting most often involve participants, location, and time of the speech act. The *contextual function* associated with the setting component is reflected in messages that tell something about the time, place, or persons in the interaction. Many linguistic forms referring to these things cannot be interpreted without reference to the speech act itself, for their meanings are not fixed but relative (e.g., "me," "you," "here," "there," "now," "then").

Try replacing the word "function" in the above paragraphs with the word "meaning." This will give you some idea of the variety of meanings or types of information that are recoverable from speech. Any component of a speech act, it should be emphasized, may contribute any of the kinds of functional meanings discussed. The functions have been assigned here to individual components on the basis of dominant associations. Whereas traditional conceptions of the linguistic system focus on the referential function, the sociolinguistic system must be seen in terms of all nine functions; nine different types of meaning are involved.

In the wider context of sociolinguistic meaning we can say that aspiration or vowel length in English, for example, make meaningful distinctions. These features are nondistinctive in English phonology with respect to the referential function, but they can clearly be distinctive in terms of expressive function, signalling different attitudes on the part of the speaker.

Sociolinguistic description with its broadened framework of speech-act components and functions has helped to revive interest in larger linguistic constructions than sentences. When we speak, for example, the internal structure of one sentence often determines the internal structure of others in the same *discourse unit* (e.g., the paragraph). Syntactic rules apply, in other words, not just to sentences and their constituents, but also to combinations of sentences.

Syntactic and phonological rules can be grouped under three distinct headings corresponding to different relationships among units. There are *rules of alternation* where a unit on one level of abstraction is represented by several on another. Phonemes are represented as allophones on a more superficial level, for example. The relationship implied here is specified by our conjunction "or." *Rules of co-occurrence* tell us which units occur in simultaneous combination with others to represent a single unit on another level of abstraction. Phonemes, for example, can also be represented as combinations of features. The relationship implied here is specified by our conjunction "and." Finally, there are *rules of sequencing* (or concatenation) which tell us how elements can be placed one after another in the formation of larger units on the same level of abstraction. Another example from phonology would be the rules arranging phonemes in a syllable. Sociolinguistic rules, it turns out, also fall into these three categories of rules.[7]

7. An absorbing treatment of sociolinguistics that isolates these rule types in a slightly different way is given by Susan Ervin-Tripp, "Sociolinguistics," in *Advances in Experimental Social Psychology*, vol. 4, ed. L. Berkowitz (New York: Academic Press, Inc., 1969), pp. 91-165.

THE ORIGIN AND EVOLUTION OF LANGUAGE
The Nature of Language

SUMMARY

Language is man's most important means of transferring ideas from one mind to another. Of all our senses, hearing best meets the demands of human interaction for receiving referential messages. Speech can take place in the dark and with the hands full. In order to make use of the hearing sense, ideas must somehow be converted to sound. Our speech organs produce the sounds into which ideas have been converted in patterned ways. This jump from idea to speech sound is based on man's ability to let one thing stand for another—called symbolization—and involves a complex organization of processes that is often referred to as linguistic structure. If we wish to consider language as only a referential system, then we can use the notion of sociolinguistic system or communicative repertoire to take into account other functions of speech. Because social factors are usually inextricably woven into linguistic constructions, we may end up having to broaden our conception of language to include what is presently seen as the sociolinguistic system. Doing so should help us to more realistically approach the origin and evolution of language.

For Further Reading

Birdwhistell, Ray L. *Kinesics and Context*. Philadelphia: University of Pennsylvania Press, 1970. A book of essays on body movement in human communication by a founder of kinesic studies. The essays include easy reading as well as technical articles.

Gumperz, John and Hymes, Dell, eds. *Directions in Sociolinguistics*. New York: Holt, Rinehart and Winston Inc., 1972. This book contains nineteen articles on ways of speaking in almost as many different societies. It has an appended guide for doing fieldwork and an excellent bibliography of sociolinguistic works.

Hymes, Dell *Foundations in Sociolinguistics*. Philadelphia: University of Pennsylvania Press, 1974. Aptly characterized by its title, this book provides a theoretical framework for sociolinguistics and gives many examples from around the world to illustrate some highly sophisticated notions.

Langacker, Ronald W. *Language and its Structure*. 2d ed. New York: Harcourt Brace Jovanovich, Inc., 1973. An excellent introduction to language and linguistics. It is well-organized and very readable.

Lyons, John *Introduction to Theoretical Linguistics*. Cambridge: Cambridge University Press, 1968. A 500 page consideration of theoretical linguistics as of 1968. Introduces most important concepts of traditional grammar and devotes considerable space to semantics.

Schane, Sanford *Generative Phonology*. Englewood Cliffs, N.J.: Prentice-Hall, Inc., 1973. Well-written introduction to modern generative phonology.

Bibliography

Bauman, Richard and Sherzer, Joel 1974. *Explorations in the Ethnography of Speaking*. London and New York: Cambridge University Press.

Bloomfield, Leonard 1933. *Language*. New York: Holt, Rinehart and Winston.

Brosnahan, L. F. and Malmberg, Bertil 1970. *Introduction to Phonetics*. Cambridge: W. Heffer & Sons Ltd.

Brown, Roger 1958. *Words and Things*. Glencoe, Ill.: The Free Press.

Burling, Robbins 1970. *Man's Many Voices*. New York: Holt, Rinehart and Winston.

Chomsky, Noam 1965. *Aspects of the Theory of Syntax*. Cambridge, Mass.: M.I.T. Press.

Heffner, R-M.S. 1960. *General Phonetics*. Madison: The University of Wisconsin Press.

Hockett, Charles F. 1958. *A Course in Modern Linguistics*. New York: The Macmillan Company.

Labov, William 1972. *Sociolinguistic Patterns.* Philadelphia: University of Pennsylvania Press.

Lehmann, Winfred P. 1972. *Descriptive Linguistics.* New York: Random House.

2 | Theories

It may surprise you to learn that the most recent bibliography of works relating to the origin of language contains some 10,000 references.[1] Yet relatively little was published on the subject in scientific journals during the first half of this century. A spate of speculations and acrimonious debates during the nineteenth century and earlier had finally led to a climate of opinion in which the origin of language was practically a taboo topic among scientists. As early as 1866 the Linguistic Society of Paris had imposed a constitutional ban on papers dealing with language origins, a ban that had to be reaffirmed in 1911. Unverifiable speculations were viewed as detrimental to linguistic science because they channeled research energy away from other important work.

In recent years the subject has been revived in technical journals. New issues have been raised, along with some old ones, sparked by advances in our knowledge concerning animal communication systems, speech and brain mechanisms, language acquisition by children, and universals of language. New techniques for linguistic reconstruction and the interpretation of archaeological materials as well as recently discovered hominid fossil remains have also contributed to the revival of scientific interest in language origins.

EARLY THEORIES OF THE ORIGIN OF LANGUAGE

Early theorists looked to the essential question of the relationship between sound and meaning for their answers. The nature of this relationship divided the ancient Greek philosophers into two camps, some believing in a *natural* connection between sound and meaning, others believing that the connection is *conventional* or arbitrary. Nineteenth-century speculations on the origin of language also reflect this split in opinions. Rationalists or nativists such as Wilhelm von Humboldt assumed the connection to be natural while empiricists such as Dwight Whitney held to the view that such connections are necessarily arbitrary. Although much has been learned about language since the nineteenth century, opinion is still divided on the question of how sound relates to meaning in language, as reflected in current debate between rationalist and empiricist traditions in linguistic theory. The lines are, however, less sharply drawn now, and some of the crucial evidential questions are different.

Most early theories see human language as developing from some natural connection

1. Gordon Hewes, *Language Origins: A Bibliography,* 2nd ed. (The Hague: Mouton, 1974).

between sound and meaning; a connection that can be seen in aspects of present-day languages and that might have been made with the presumably simpler mental equipment of the earliest men.

Sound Mimicry Theory

This theory proposes that human speech originated when the earliest humans began to imitate natural sounds, sounds present in their environment, and sounds made by animals in particular. Sounds of nature would have included bird songs, rushing water, whistling wind, thunder, chirping of insects, animal calls, and the sounds of eating, sneezing, coughing, urinating, and defecating. Humans and birds especially seem to have rather well developed abilities to imitate many environmental sounds, especially sounds made by other animals, and this ability could well have been very useful to protohominids (early man) for luring game. Could sounds used by protohominids to lure game or mimic sounds of nature come to represent the game or other objects in nature in the minds of these prelinguistic humans? Could the processes of sound change that operate in present day language have led to onomatopoetic words in earlier times that would conjure up conceptual representations of environmental stimuli even when the stimuli themselves were not present?[2]

Most, perhaps all, languages of today make use of onomatopoeia. That is, their vocabularies contain words that bear a sound resemblance to sounds associated with animals and other natural phenomena. Think of our own words for cuckoo, sneeze, splash, growl, and so on. On the other hand, few languages make extensive use of onomatopoeia. Moreover, many onomatopoetic words found in various languages seem to have attained their present form relatively recently. The proposition that onomatopoeia or sound imitation was a principal source of words in the earliest language has been variously designated the *bow-wow theory* and the *onomatopoeia theory,* and it has had many famous supporters. Arguments for this proposition are perhaps more convincing than those advanced against it, but whether true or not the theory tells us very little about the origin of language.

Interjection Theory

Labelled the *pooh-pooh theory* by Max Müller in the nineteenth century, the interjection theory proposes that the first words in human language developed from involuntary expressive sounds made by prelinguistic man—sounds emitted spontaneously as reactions to surprise, pain, relief, pleasure, anger, etc. We have many interjections in English that are conventionalized expressions based on involuntarily emitted sounds (e.g., ow!, whee!, oops!, oh!, huh?, yecchh!, and so on). The theory is that earlier involuntary sounds came to have more than simply expressive significance, and that they began at some point to make reference to actions that normally would have elicited them. As with the sound mimicry theory, the interjection theory implies that reference through naming by means of a preexisting repertoire of sounds constituted the first linguistic step.

Ding-Dong Theory

The *ding-dong theory,* so-called by Max Müller, seeks to explain the origin of lan-

2. That sound change operates in bird song can be inferred from the discovery of dialect variation in some species. Furthermore dialect differentiation may not be purely a genetic matter as evidenced by studies on song acquisition in birds. See Fernando Nottebohm, "The Origins of Vocal Learning," *The American Naturalist* 106 (1972):116-40. If sound change operates in bird song, why not in human mimicry?

guage by positing a law of harmony in nature whereby everything has its own inherent sound which is perceivable under the appropriate circumstances, in much the same way that a bell rings when it is struck. In a manner analogous to the elicitation of sound when an object is struck, so humans are "struck" when they perceive objects and events in nature, according to this theory. Thus a man seeing a tree fall will be metaphorically struck by the event and will emit the naturally evoked words "the tree falls." Another version of this theory is that man is gifted with the ability to somehow perceive the natural and inherent sounds of objects—sounds that are liberated when the objects are struck—and to imitate these sounds thus creating words. Now, it is true that all objects have their own natural frequencies of vibration, and that these vibrations can be elicited by vibrations of nearby objects. It seems, however, that the facts of language diversification and variation do not support either interpretation of the ding-dong theory.

Work Chant Theory

The work chant theory, humorously christened the *yo-he-ho theory,* links communal work to the origin of speech. According to this theory, groups of early humans, straining with the intense and common effort necessary to move a fallen log or other such occupation, came to emit spontaneous grunts which were partly consonantal and which would eventually be used to signal common exertion in much the same way that today we use "heave" or "pull" in group lifting or pulling efforts. Eventually the grunts used for coordinating the efforts of many persons in a rhythmic way came to be associated with the work performed and then to stand for the work itself in symbolic communication. Ludwig Noiré, one of the proponents of this theory, also saw

speech sounds arising from imitation of noises made by tools at work.

Gesture Theory

The suggestion that gesture language preceded speech is very old, and among its supporters are some of the biggest names in philosophy and nineteenth-century anthropology. It is easy to imagine bipedal animals gesturing to attract attention or pointing out a particular object with a wave of the hand. Perhaps you can even visualize a group of prelinguistic humans imitating the shapes of things with hand gestures or pointing to parts of the body. Association of the gesture with the thing indicated would then have to be extended to situations in which the object was not present. If such pre-linguistic-gestural symbolization were to evolve in man, it could have provided a base—perhaps even of propositional communication through hand and arm movements—that might later be transferred to the vocal-auditory channel. Gesture language would have been limited in use by visibility conditions, and this might have stimulated the development of audible speech for overcoming that handicap. Any elaboration of gestural communication would certainly demand good motor control of arms and fingers, but initial development of such a system would not have stringent motor requirements.

A gesture language would probably have to be largely iconic and gesturally onomatopoetic, which might make for an extremely large and cumbersome vocabulary because so many items and objects would eventually need to be named. These would provide two more reasons for adapting vocal noises for communication. Gesture preceding language is a promising speculation, and such a theory can account in terms of selective advantages for a gradual growth of linguistic capacity from the perspectives of brain development and modifications of the vocal tract for speech. Early gesture theorists have no more plausible explanations for the mental jump from expressive to referential communication than do proponents of the other early theories considered. Gordon Hewes has recently revived and augmented the theory that gesture language preceded spoken language in a series of carefully researched articles.[3]

Mouth-Gesture Theory

The mouth-gesture theory assumes that the first human language was purely gestural and seeks to explain the shift to a vocal-auditory system by positing a time when manual gestures were unconsciously copied by positions and movements of the mouth, lips, and tongue. In combination with air expelled through the vocal tract, these unconscious gestures would be made audible and could be recognized as alternative symbols of reference. Increasing sophistication subsequently led these primitive speakers to further conventionalize their speech sounds by limiting movements to up-and-down and back-and-forth. Called by some the *ta-ta theory*, its most recent elaboration has been by Richard Paget in several publications.[4]

Singing Theory

Speech originated in song according to this theory. Birds sing, but among the primates only man can sing. Song (without words, of course) is potentially capable of signalling a great deal of information by recombining notes (analogous to phonemes), which are meaningless by themselves, in various ways to form measures with meaning (analogous to words). Hypothetically, measures could be arranged syntacti-

cally to create whole songs (analogous to sentences). Each note could consist of distinctive features taken only from the three variable dimensions of pitch, length, and stress. Vocal equipment necessary for singing may require nearly as much control and specialization, however, as is necessary for speech. In the final analysis there is probably no good reason to consider singing any simpler to produce or discriminate than the sounds of speech, and the absence of singing in our primate cousins should be viewed as evidence against rather than for the singing theory.

Babbling Theory

Human infants babble, creating sounds apparently spontaneously and to no particular purpose. On the assumption that pre-linguistic-hominid infants also went through a similar babbling period, the babbling theory proposes that babbling sounds at one point became associated with specific elements of the environment, and individual sounds or syllables came to stand for the environmental features to which they were associated. Referential function in this manner came to replace what originally functioned expressively. One subscriber to this theory believes that both babbling and the capacity to symbolize came about through mutation, and their co-occurrence inevitably resulted in language.

This sampling of early theories about language origins gives some idea of the sorts of speculations that have been advanced. There are many others, both old and new,

3. See Gordon Hewes, "Primate Communication and the Gestural Origin of Language," *Current Anthropology* 14 (1973):5-24.

4. See, for example, Richard Paget, *Human Speech* (London: Routledge and Kegan Paul, 1963). This is a reissue of his nineteenth-century book.

seeking to explain and reconstruct that magic moment, or era, when language was born. This century has witnessed its own group of theories that will be sampled in somewhat greater detail here.

LATER THEORIES

Cooperation Theory

In 1927 Grace de Laguna presented a plausible and cogently argued treatise, stressing what she viewed as the fundamental function of speech—the coordination of activities in social groups. Her book *Speech: Its Function and Development* argues that human cooperation was accomplished through the development of three primary forms of speech behavior: the question, the command, and the declaration. Each of these arose through progressive differentiation from prototypical aspects of prehominid vocalizations, referred to generically as "the animal cry."

The animal cry is merely one element in a larger integrated total physical response to environmental stimuli affecting the animal's emotions. Speech differs from the animal cry in that speech may be elicited by objects and events of only indirect interest and little emotional value for the speaker, and it may constitute more nearly the totality of an individual's response in a given situation. If the cry represents only a small portion of the hypothetical prehominid's fairly fixed and emotion laden response to directly perceived contextual elements such as the arrival of a predator, then the transition to sentential speech must have involved a gradual loss of emotional loading in vocal messages and a gradual increase in vocal coding of contextual variables. Both of these processes result in increased indirectness of means by which the organism deals with and relates to its objective environment; and both of these processes stemmed naturally from a developing ne-

cessity among the prelinguistic hominids for calling attention to varied and specific properties of objects. In short, the need arose for *predication*.

If the subject of a proposition is something that possesses a number of unspecified attributes, predication is then the specification of one or more relevant attributes from among those which have not yet been specified. We might just as well use the terms "topic" and "comment" in place of "subject" and "predicate." De Laguna happens to use the term "predication." An example may clarify this simple notion of predication and show how a social animal could benefit from an ability to communicate predicatively.

Imagine a protohominid group that has spread out to look for food. Imagine further that along comes a potentially dangerous predator, say a lion, unnoticed by most of the group. One member notices the predator, gives a cry of alarm, and then retreats along with the rest to a position of safety. By responding immediately and emotionally to the warning, the group has followed a single course of action and temporarily forfeited their ability to gather food, regardless of whether or not the predator was hungry and constituted an actual danger. Moreover, some members of the group might well have retreated unknowingly right into the lion's path and gotten killed. But what if the individual who gave the alarm had been able to communicate specifically what kind of predator had been sensed (for predators differ in hunting habits and in the degree of danger they represent), what direction it was coming from, how far away it was, how hungry it looked, whether it was alone, and so on? And what if the members of the group were capable of suppressing their immediate emotional flight response in order to act more intelligently in terms of the particular situation and on the basis of information received from their fellow? Surely in the long run this would result in less time and energy wasted on unwarranted retreats, and in fewer deaths caused by predictable retreat patterns. Continued survival of the group, then, is more adequately guaranteed by the ability of individuals to send and interpret more specific information about the environment, and also by their ability to delay their emotional responses to situations.[5] Predicative communication confers a selective advantage for survival on the group in which it can be effectively utilized. The most primitive predication can be communicated either gesturally by pointing or vocally by naming, each mode having its own distinct advantages. In either case information must be both transmitted and received to benefit the group.

De Laguna suggests that at some point the predicative cry of protohominids might be termed a sentence-word very similar in some respects to the *holophrastic* or one-word utterance of a one-year-old human child. Both depend completely on perceptual context. More specifically, unlike adult human sentences, the protohominid sentence-word and the child's holophrastic utterance are both capable of functioning alone without the aid of other words; both are characterized by looseness and fluidity of significance; and the meanings of both are determined by the particular context of each separate occasion in which they are used. Correlatively, the sender and receiver(s) need to be perceptually present together in the situation.

If there is a selective advantage to predicatively coordinating complex and varied behavior in specific situations and a further advantage to coordinating action beyond the limits of the common perceptually present situation, it might follow to expect a progressive differentiation of sentence-words as an increasing selection of environmental features came to be encoded in these sentence-words. That is, there would be more sentence-words; and as their number increased, their meanings would become progressively more fixed and specific.

According to de Laguna's speculations, as the objects of human action came to play different roles in different situations, different properties—and actions with respect to these properties—took on importance for determining behavior toward the objects. Thus, as the terms of primitive language became more fixed and definite, these sentence-words became correspondingly incapable of functioning alone because the name of an object had to be distinguished from its attributes and from acts related to it. The use of a name had to be supplemented by a term capable of specifying a particular act demanded by the occasion.

From the sentence-word, then, developed the multiword utterance, the sentence. De Laguna suggests that the earliest full sentences might have had an "isolating type" of structure, where constituent words do not belong to fixed parts of speech in that they may serve as noun, verb, adjective, or adverb without internal modification or affixing, and where sequential order signals part-of-speech relationships as well as others such as subject-object.

The cooperation theory propounded by de Laguna does not tie stages in the evolution of human language to any proposed sequence of fossil hominids, although she mentions in passing that, contrary to prevailing opinion of the time, Neanderthal Man must have had vocal language. Further, she sees the protohominid descent from the trees to the savannas during the Pliocene as a precipitating factor in glottogenesis. Mobile, social, and manually dexterous animals well adapted to arboreal life were

5. As a child were you ever told to count to ten before expressing any anger? Present-day humans have to learn to suppress immediate emotional responses as they grow up.

faced in a savanna context with many new behavioral options as well as new dangers. Emotional type-responses to situations had to give way to many new context determined reactions. Tools, hunting, and predicative communication were interrelated and mutually reinforcing elements functioning to increase the range and extent of cooperative action in the group's struggle for survival.

Contact Theory

Another theory of glottogenesis comes from the work of Géza Révész, who focuses on a different function of speech in society, that of social contact. For him it was an instinctive organismic need for copresence with like organisms, followed by a need to express and share emotions, and eventually joined by an impulse for intellectual contact, from which linguistic communication developed.

Satisfaction of these increasing social needs shows an evolutionary sequence in the development of verbal forms from nonverbal ones, and this sequence is manifested in the cry, the call, and the word. The cry expresses little more than inner excitement, the call additionally expresses demands for particular action, and the word creates an ability to make imperative, indicative, and interrogative modes vocally explicit. A transition stage between prelanguage and primitive language with its three modes is postulated by Révész, who feels that before statements and questions evolved language forms were essentially commands.

Révész, a German psychologist with a broad range of interests, devoted many years to formulating his ideas on glottogenesis. His approach to the subject is more logical than empirical and suffers from pedantic verbosity as well as from a lack of sustaining evidence for most of his assumptions. The first third of his book *The Origins*

and Prehistory of Language is nevertheless an interesting critique and classification of previous theories.

Verb Theory

In 1959 A. S. Diamond, a lawyer by profession, published *The History and Origin of Language*. In it he painstakingly presents a wealth of somewhat uncritically examined and selected data from a variety of sources, and arrives at some rather concrete conclusions about the nature of the very earliest language and how it later evolved. The evidence is used to establish (1) the growth of parts of speech from the single primitive verb root; (2) the earliest function of language; (3) the phonological shapes of the earliest words; and (4) the meanings of the earliest words.

In brief, language is said to have originated in requests for assistance from one male to another in early, local, seminomadic groups. These requests took the form of imperative verbs referring to actions requiring maximum bodily effort (e.g., break, cut, kill, smash): actions that a lone man might need help in performing. The original imperatives were vaguer in reference and more emotive in content than today's verbs, and they employed loudly pronounced syllables consisting of stops or nasal consonants followed by the vowel "*a*" (e.g., ba, ka, ma). These syllables and their posited meanings are not unlike the nine fundamental words set forth by Alexander Murray in 1823.

Diamond's book makes fascinating reading. His arguments are simple and elegant, and all lead, if uncritically accepted, to just about the same conclusion: the verb is the foundation on which language is built. Increasing linguistic and cultural sophisication witnessed the later arrival of nouns and then adjectives. We are shown this by means of word counts. First, Shakespearian texts show a preponderance of verbs among the most frequently appearing words. Among the less commonly used words there is an increase in proportion of nouns, and among the least frequent there is a rise in the proportion of adjectives—verbs, of course, suffer correspondingly. Then word counts on samples of English literature from 1400 through the present lead to a similar picture diachronically, with the percentage of verbs falling off as the percentage of nouns and then adjectives increases. Next, the comparative linguistic approach, but here the languages of technologically backward hunting and gathering peoples are taken to represent language at the end of the Paleolithic when compared with modern English. Counts then establish that while verbs represent less than 10 percent of English words, they constitute some 50 percent of the words in late Paleolithic languages. Extrapolating from here, the conclusion is reached that at one time language had only verbs, and that the evolution of vocabulary reflects the addition of other parts of speech in successive stages.

Diamond finds further evidence of this process in the morphological history of individual words in English. For example he sees "nationalistic" in terms of successive additions of suffixes deriving different parts of speech from the original Latin *na* ("to be born"). "Na-(verb)-tion(noun)-al(adj.)-is (verb)-t(noun)-ic(adj.), the first three terms of the series being of Latin form, and the last three from the Greek through the French." In this manner one can peel off the outer and most recent layers to reveal the original verb root, and notice in microcosmic form the cyclical process of vocabulary formation: again revealing successive additions of nouns and then adjectives to verbs in a vocabulary as well as the cyclical creation of nouns and then adjectives from verbs.

More data is produced by Diamond, which he accepts as indicating that a universal feature of present-day languages is that the verb in its imperative modality is uninflected, having no affixes attached to the base form. Thus the imperative of the verb, expressing a request for action is suggested as the earliest form and content of language. The facts are wrong here, however, for many languages inflect verbs for the imperative mode by means of affixes, for example Tzeltal.

The phonological forms of the earliest words is derived by Diamond from studies of the physiology of speech production (easiest sounds are the earliest), of phonological universals (most common sounds worldwide are the earliest), and of language acquisition (first sounds learned by children are the earliest). From all three sources, based on the assumptions in parentheses, it would appear that the earliest words were syllables of a nasal or stop consonant followed by the single vowel *a*.

Finally, drawing on primate studies and on meaning changes in the history of words, Diamond infers the content of the earliest words, concluding that they were requests for assistance in physically demanding efforts.

An altogether entertaining book to read, *The History and Origin of Language* is strong on methods and techniques of inference, but weak on data reliability and conclusions.

Morris Swadesh's Theory

Morris Swadesh is the only contemporary professional linguist that I know of who has set forth his ideas on glottogenesis in book form. Swadesh, whose many contributions have been fundamental to present conceptions of language, put his detailed knowledge of language change and linguistic reconstruction together with his creative—if daring and controversial—insight to produce *The Origin and Diversification of Language* which was edited and published posthumously in 1971.

This book proposes to divide the development of language into four major periods roughly coinciding with the dawn stone age (Eolithic) of archaeologists, the old stone age (Paleolithic), the new stone age (Neolithic), and the recent or historical period comprising the last 10,000 years.

1. The *eoglottic,* earliest period in the sequence, began 3 million years ago or more during which time *Australopithecus* roamed in the African woodlands and savannas. Prior to this time the prelinguistic ancestors of man had a system of vocal exclamations whereby a single root "word" perhaps could be modified in meaning by instinctively produced changes in loudness, length, voice quality, pitch, and patterns of repetition. They also evolved a separate imitative system in which mouth shapes more or less consciously copied the shapes and sounds of objects. Rounded lips, for example, were used for imitating round objects. The eoglottic period began when the exclamatory system was differentiated into expressive messages and demonstrative ones. There may have been only two root words whose meanings were modified by changes of rhythm, tone, point and manner of articulation, and glottal accompaniment.

2. The *paleoglottic* period saw an expansion of symbolism, used to modify meanings of a slightly expanded root vocabulary for the most part, in which symbolic significance was attached to major points and manners of articulation. Labial articulation may have expressed relative distance from speaker and velar articulation relative closeness. Glottalization could have represented quickness or abruptness, nasalization contentment, aspiration continuing energy, and voicing friendliness or affection.

3. By the *neoglottic* period a few independent roots with more or less fixed meanings had crystallized out of earlier forms inflected by sound symbolistic consonant and vowel alternations, and came to be modified in meaning by affixes. Most inflection, however, remained internal and consisted of semantically modifying a phonemic inventory consisting of /a, p, t, č, k, kʷ, h, m, n, n, w, y/ by means of rounding, fronting, backing, glottalization, or aspiration. The inflectional categories signalled by these modifications probably were those of shape, intensity, activity, proximity, repetition, and weight rather than the tense, number, gender, and so on that we associate with inflection today. During this same period binary counting began.

4. The *historical* period saw the development of digital counting, affixation to signal stem classes or parts of speech, and color terms from the names of objects. *Local languages* similar to those of preliterate peoples today gave rise to the *classic languages* of early kingdoms and empires, and in turn to *world languages* characteristic of complex societies spanning oceans and continents. World languages have the largest vocabularies, local languages the smallest. World languages have the largest proportion of nouns to verbs, local languages the smallest. World languages have the greatest variety in syllable structure, local languages the least. World languages make little use of vowel or consonant alternation for inflection; local languages make much use of such alternation, but also employ affixes and reduplication for inflecting grammatical categories.

Apart from his formulation of periods in language history, an important contention of Swadesh is that all languages in the world today are monogenetic, having evolved from a single language of the Paleolithic period; perhaps the Middle Paleolithic when *Homo sapiens neanderthalensis* (Neanderthal Man) was still around.

TWO RECENT SUGGESTIONS

Charles Hockett has suggested a plausible mechanism by which a closed call system, such as our distant ancestors may have had, could have been opened up and made productive using acoustic contours already present in the call system. This mechanism, which he refers to as *blending*, is common enough in today's language: for example the word "liger" referring to the offspring of a lion and a tiger, or the word "sparsity" which blends the forms and meanings of "sparseness" and "scarcity."

Imagine, to use Hockett's example, that a closed protohominid call system contains the redundantly encoded AB sequence signifying "food" as well as a sequence CD signifying "danger." It is conceivable that one of our ancestors seeing both stimuli at the same time could utter the blend AC and be understood by a listener to mean both "food and danger," since elements of both calls are present. By virtue of AC's new meaning, AB and CD could come to acquire the new meanings "food without danger" and "danger without food" respectively. The three calls AB, CD, and AC could then be decomposed into smaller elements with individual distinctive meanings: A for "food," B for "no danger," C for "danger," and D for "no food." In this manner, given that blends were both produced and understood, a closed system might have opened up to admit new messages. Moreover, the division into smaller meaningful segments would necessitate closer attention to acoustic detail both in production and comprehension of messages—a survival premium placed on articulatory skill and auditory discrimination.

Few people would think that silence might be significant in the origin of speech. One anthropologist has proposed that it was. Simplified, the argument runs something like this. Emotions and their vocal expression are associated with a "primitive" portion of the brain, the limbic area. The cortical area, highly developed in humans, is associated with propositional speech and the suppression of immediate emotional responses derived from the limbic area. Now, it seems that for helpless infant chimpanzees, immediate vocal responses to emotional situations could be very disadvantageous; among other things spontaneous or other limbically controlled vocalizations might attract the attention of hungry predators. Chimpanzees in fact remain relatively silent until social maturation, after which time they become quite vocal. Pressures of natural selection may well have caused a developmental retardation of limbically expressed calls in the chimpanzee and, by analogy, in our hominid ancestors. If at a later stage in evolution selective advantages for vocalization in infancy and youth accrued to the ancestral population, voluntary cortical inhibition of the already programmed inhibitory limbic circuits might have developed; remember that evolution is not reversible, so we could not expect simply to lose an already developed limbic circuit for vocal suppression. Cortically controlled inhibitory circuits associated also with delayed gratification do appear in the neocortex of modern man, particularly in the prefrontal lobe of the brain. Essentially this means voluntary control of vocalization, and also of silence.

Interestingly enough, and relevant to this hypothesis, in human societies where the role of silence has been investigated, situations where silence is specifically the norm happen also to be situations of great emotional significance for the participants. This is true for the Cuna of Panama, the Western Apache, and the Tzeltal among others.

SUMMARY

A variety of theories, actually hypotheses and speculations, have been introduced in this chapter. None of them are provable, and several of them are not disprovable either. Several of them point very clearly to an ability to symbolize, to make a mental connection between two unrelated things so that one can stand for the other, as crucial to language. Others have pointed to the need for inhibitory neural mechanisms in the brain that can prevent immediate stereotyped emotional responses to environmental stimuli. Still others emphasized man's social nature, imitative ability, or gestural capabilities. A couple of the theories attempted to work backwards in reconstructing the form and content of man's earliest linguistic utterances. None of the theories is completely satisfying, but the ideas that I personally favor come from the work of de Laguna and Swadesh. Three vital areas have not been dealt with adequately in any of the theories. Firstly, neural evolution involving some structural reorganization of the brain was necessary for language. What sort of neural evolution and how many genetic changes were involved remains a mystery almost untouched by the theories. Secondly, the vocal apparatus of man has undergone considerable change in the past couple of million years, most notably, one suspects, in pharyngeal configuration and tongue control. Little has been said yet on this subject, but it will be reintroduced in chapter 5. Suffice it to say here, man's fine articulatory control would probably not have developed in the absence of propositional speech. And finally, adaptive advantages of neural evolution with respect to both articulatory control and perception-ideation capacities must be posited at all stages in the evolution of language. For the earliest stages in particular we need to posit a perhaps unique environmental niche to which prelinguistic man brought unique physical and mental characteristics. The nature of these niches and characteristics have not sufficiently been spelled out yet.

For Further Reading

Chafe, Wallace *Meaning and the Structure of Language*. Chicago: The University of Chi-

cago Press, 1970. The whole book is an appealing semantically based theory of language. Part one presents a hypothetical sequence of language evolution cast in the framework of Chafe's theory.

Hockett, Charles and Ascher, Robert "The Human Revolution." *Current Anthropology* 5 (1964):135-47. This is a cleverly written piece on protohominid environment and early developments in language as well as other aspects of culture.

Lancaster, Jane "Primate Communication Systems and the Emergence of Human Languages," in *Primates*, ed. by Phyllis Jay. New York: Holt, Rinehart and Winston, 1968, pp. 439-57.

Wescott, Roger, ed. *Language Origins*. Silver Spring, Md.: Linstok Press, 1974. This book resulted from a symposium on language origins held in 1972. Included are six excellent articles and several excellent commentaries on the articles, in addition to a forty-seven page selected bibliography on glottogenesis. Some of the reading requires linguistic sophistication.

Bibliography

Darwin, Charles R. 1888. *The Descent of Man and Selection in Relation to Sex*. 2d ed. New York: D. Appleton and Company.

Diamond, A. S. 1959. *The History and Origin of Language*. New York: Philosophical Library.

Hale, Horatio 1887. "The Origin of Language and the Antiquity of Speaking Man." *Proceedings of the American Association for the Advancement of Science* 35:279-323.

Hewes, Gordon 1973. "Primate Communication and the Gestural Origin of Language." *Current Anthropology* 14:5-24.

Jesperson, Otto 1922. *Language, Its Nature, Development and Origin*. London: G. Allen & Unwin.

de Laguna, Grace Andrus 1963. *Speech, Its Function and Development*. Bloomington:

Indiana University Press (first published in 1927).

Noiré, Ludwig 1917. *The Origin and Philosophy of Language*. 2d ed. Chicago: The Open Court Publishing Company.

Paget, Richard 1956. "The Origins of Language, With Special Reference to the Paleolithic Age." *Journal of World History* 1:399-414.

Peters, Charles R. 1972. "Evolution of the Capacity for Language: a New Start on an Old Problem." *Man* 7:33-49.

Révész, Géza 1956. *The Origins and Prehistory of Language*. New York: Philosophical Library.

Swadesh, Morris 1971. *The Origin and Diversification of Language*. Chicago: Aldine-Atherton, Inc.

3 | Issues

Think of all the questions that you might ask about language origins! When, for example, did the genesis of language occur, and where? Was there only a single original language from which all others diversified? Did gesture language come before spoken language? What biological equipment of our ancestors was instrumental in glottogenesis, and in what ways? How did tools, diet, and bipedalism contribute to language origins? What was the natural environment of the protohominids as they were about to cross the linguistic threshold? Was language created by gradual growth or by a sudden evolutionary jump? Could Neanderthals speak? Did the Australopithecines have any sort of vocal language? Was preadaptation involved in a shift from nonlanguage to language? What was communication like before language? What is the evolutionary relationship between capacity to think and capacity to use language? Is chimpanzee communication of today at all comparable to protohominid communication? Is language continuing to evolve even now?

The answers to these questions and to many more are still being debated today, even as new evidence bearing on them arrives. Some issues will probably focus debate for some time to come. Scientific consensus may be reached on others in the not too distant future. Let us take a selection of issues here, and try to expose some of their salient points.

WHEN?

When did language come into being? The answer here depends, of course, on what formal characteristics you choose to define into language. One alternative is to take Roger Brown's description from chapter 1, recalling that meaningless sounds must be combined in different ways to comprise morphemes with meaning that also combine in different ways to make up interpretable sentences with propositional meanings that are not always reducible to a summation of constituent morpheme meanings. But defining language is not enough. The answer also depends upon archaeological evidence including remnants of fossil men.

To begin with, language must go back at least five thousand years to the time of early city-states in the Near East. There is already evidence of writing systems by that time, so there had to be language. If pottery making implies speech, we can go back even further; pottery more than ten thousand years old has been found in Japan. More than twenty thousand years ago fired clay figurines were being made; their makers probably spoke.

Scratchings made on bone dated around thirty thousand years ago have recently been subjected to microscopic analysis and interpreted as a lunar calendar of Cro-Magnon Man. A fascinating story of scientific detective work lies behind this discovery, which pushes the origin of language back at least to Upper Paleolithic times.

More indirect evidence for speech in the Upper Paleolithic comes from Cro-Magnon cave paintings and outlines of left hands which points to right-handedness in the population. Right-handedness goes with dominance of the left half of the brain which in turn is related to cerebral specialization for speech.

Homo sapiens sapiens, called Cro-Magnon in Europe, first appears about forty thousand years ago. Most anthropologists are confident that language goes back that far. Fewer are willing to credit *Homo sapiens neanderthalensis* with speech capabilities approaching our own in complexity. There is, however, some fragmentary evidence here for spoken language. The upper-left to lower-right diagonal scratches found on the front teeth of some Neanderthal specimens could indicate right-handed stone knife wielders cutting off protruding scraps from mouthfuls of meat—cerebral hemispheric dominance again. Similarly, wounds on the left sides of several Neanderthals could have been caused by encounters between right-handed opponents. Moreover, ritual burials of Neanderthals found in Europe and the Near East have been interpreted as expressions of belief in an afterlife, and this suggests speech.

Neanderthal populations arose more than 100,000 years ago and apparently disappeared with the coming of Cro-Magnon. Before Neanderthal there was *Pithecanthropus,* now classiifed as *Homo erectus,* who emerged about a million years ago, first in Africa and South Asia, then expanding to populate the temperate zones. He controlled fire, organized large-scale elephant hunts, and may have had some linguistic skills. The last assumption is made on the basis of some plaster casts of the inside of fossil skulls which show cerebral elaboration of the motor speech area.

Preceding *Homo erectus* there was *Australopithecus,* remains of which go back as far as 4 million years ago. Prior to that, in Pliocene times, *Ramapithecus* extends to about 12 million years ago. *Australopithecus* fashioned crude pebble tools, had a brain slightly larger than that of a chimpanzee, and probably walked on two legs. Few anthropologists attribute language to *Australopithecus,* and fewer are willing to even speculate about his predecessor, *Ramapithecus,* with barely more than a few fossil teeth to go on.

WHERE?

Where did language come into being? This ultimately depends on answers to the last question, but it is possible, nevertheless, to limit the locations under consideration by looking at the distribution of fossil hominids. Man did not enter the Americas, for example, until 40,000 years ago according to some investigators, and a more conservative estimate based on available dating techniques puts the figure at closer to 15,000 years. Language probably didn't originate there. A look at the distribution of fossil finds, in fact, presents an interesting picture of ancestral populations expanding through time from a geographic area that includes first East Africa and Northwest India (*Ramapithecus*), then adding South Africa and Java (*Australopithecus*), later including the Atlantic coasts of Europe and Africa as well as China (*erectus,* Neanderthal), and finally the rest of the world (Modern Man). The midpoint for each of these successive configurations seems to lie

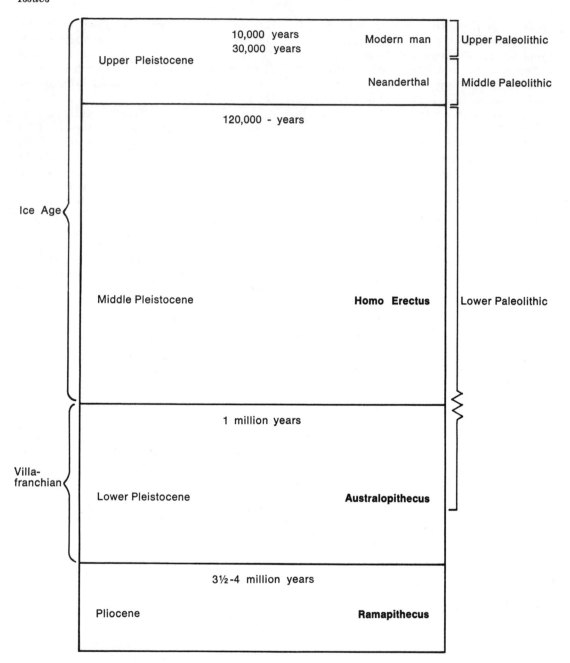

Figure 3.1 ANTECEDENTS OF MAN

in the Near East, although very early hominids have not yet been recovered from that focal area.

If we decide that language first emerged in the Upper Paleolithic among Cro-Magnon types, then glottogenesis can be attributed to a core area around the Mediterranean. Similarly if it happened in the Middle Paleolithic among Neanderthals. For *erectus* or *Australopithecus*, it is more difficult to arrive at a single focus in that area because of scanty fossil evidence, but the possibility cannot be ruled out.

On the basis of linguistic evidence, Morris Swadesh also sees the Near East as a key region—as a hub from which the world's major linguistic groupings radiate out like spokes in a rough analogy to the Biblical story of the Tower of Babel. The where of linguistic origins, in sum, may be a less open question than many others.

MONOGENESIS OR POLYGENESIS?

One thing we can be sure of. At present there are several thousand separate languages in the world, whereas at some earlier point in time there were fewer. In fact, there must be a point in prehistoric times when there were no languages at all. The issue here is whether all current languages of the world are descendants of a single common ancestor (monogenesis) or from several independent sources (polygenesis). Was language created once or many times?

Swadesh devised an ingenious method for establishing the monogenesis theory as correct, assuming that similarities above the chance level between two widely separated "unrelated" languages such as Spanish and Aztec could only be explained on the basis of historical retention. Using a 100 word basic list for each language, he first established an index of chance similarity between the two languages by comparing each word on one list for resemblance to each word on the other list. Among the 10,000 word pairs that were thus compared, about 3 percent showed resemblances. Then he compared only words with essentially the same meaning between the two languages, reasoning that if these 100 comparisons showed resemblances of greater than 3 percent, then the pairs with equivalent forms and meaning are probably related.

Swadesh found that his comparisons of synonyms between the two languages gave a greater percentage of similarity than could be attributed to chance. He also reasoned that if all languages are ultimately related, the older the Old World language that he compared with Aztec, the greater the discrepancy between percentage of synonymous forms showing resemblances and percentage derived from the index of chance similarity. Comparisons between Latin and Aztec, and then the even older Hittite and Aztec, showed that this was indeed the case; discrepancies became greater the farther back in time he went for one of the languages to be compared.

One could object to Swadesh's "proof" of monogenesis on the grounds that the historical retention which he demonstrated might have come about through words that were originally borrowed from one language by another and then retained in the daughter languages. It is also possible that the greater than chance level similarities reflect language universals showing up in vocabulary because of an underlying unity of the human mind rather than genetic relatedness of the languages. Monogenesis versus polygenesis is still an unresolved issue perhaps, but Swadesh's method for deciding it is interesting and provocative.

BIOLOGICAL AND BEHAVIORAL PREREQUISITES

What biological and behavioral characteristics of prelinguistic hominids were instrumental to the development of language, and how do they interrelate evolutionarily? This is one of the most difficult questions of all. First, if we don't know for sure which hominids were first developing language, it is hard to decide which behavioral patterns and morphological characteristics, attributed to particular hominid populations on the basis of archaeological evidence, to select for association with language. Second, even if we could pinpoint the time of language emergence, it is very difficult to unravel the extremely complex causal interrelationships among language, diet, teeth, tool types, brain size and organization, bipedalism, throwing ability, social organization, and so on, not to mention interaction of these characteristics with the natural environment. Third, the fossil and archaeological record is so scanty and sporadic that most inferences drawn about any of these things are highly tentative; educated guesses you might say.

Nevertheless, several trends show up in our limited record of hominid development; trends which give a gross picture of biological and behavioral changes that we know resulted at some point in linguistic man. Brain size increased from about 500 cc in *Australopithecus* through 1,000 cc in *erectus* to about a 1,500 cc average in Neanderthal after which it remained about the same (perhaps declining slightly) up through the present. Hominids walked upright by the time of *Australopithecus,* and gradually refined their bipedal efficiency. Bipedalism allows for the carrying of food, weapons, tools, and babies without necessarily hampering locomotion very much. Seen by some as an outgrowth of charging behavior—like that of chimpanzees and gorillas—bipedalism has also been attributed to the need for seeing over tall savanna grass, to efficiency in the pursuit of game, or to wading ever deeper in the water while evading predators and gathering shellfish. Reduction in the size of canines came very early and has been

viewed as an adaptive response to seed eating which requires back and forth jaw motions, to their being made unnecessary by tools and weapons, or to social group living where they could be dangerous to other group members.

Other biological trends for which little concrete evidence exists, but which we assume were important in hominid evolution, were increasing refinement of the hand's manipulatory ability, increasing hand-eye coordination, increasing lateralization of the brain (i.e., functional differentiation of the cerebral hemispheres), decreasing proportion of wired-in or instinctive reflexes, increasingly long period from birth to sexual maturity because learning takes place during this period, and decreasing cyclicity in sexual activities.

Behavioral characteristics commonly associated with the development of language include tool-use and tool-making, hunting, and the use of fire. These are interrelated activities, and each can imply many other aspects of the social life of early man. Hunting could have been instrumental in encouraging bipedalism so that weapons could be carried and used effectively, and the fruits of the hunt transported. It would have encouraged such cooperative behavior as food sharing, sexual division of labor, pair bonding, and incest taboos. Each group could have ranged over a wider area than if they were vegetarian foragers and they could have maintained semipermanent campsites. Hunters would have had to suppress dominance displays and other agressive behavior in certain contexts, and the hunting life would seem to encourage planning, forethought, memory, and tradition. Many observers have felt that the role of hunting in early man's economic life has been grossly overplayed, however, and they point to the large dependence on vegetable materials in the life of present-day hunters and gatherers.

Control of fire is useful for cooking, warmth, light, and for stampeding game animals among other things. There is evidence that *erectus* already had fire and used it in these ways. Cooking can benefit from various kinds of tools, as can hunting. Hearthstones, knives, and skinning tools are most obvious here. Toolmaking and tool use involve skills that make adaptive the kind of intelligence which we associate with language. Tools make man less directly dependent on his environment, and they put him in less direct contact with it.

The nature of tools that we find in association with fossil hominids gives some interesting hints about linguistic abilities in their makers. The pebble tools of *Australopithecus*, for example, would not seem to imply any high degree of manual skill or intelligence. Nor are the hand-axes, cleavers, and simple flake tools of *erectus* necessarily indicative of language. The Mousterian tool tradition of Neanderthal may be another story though. One anthropologist conducted an experiment, trying to teach two groups of people to make good reproductions in flint of some Mousterian tools. With one group he explained how he was making the demonstration tools; with the other he remained silent. From the interesting results of this experiment he concluded that transmission of Neanderthal tool-making techniques requires language. By the time we get to Cro-Magnon there is no longer much question about his having language. All available evidence points in that direction.

NATURAL ENVIRONMENT

If we attribute the origin of language to about forty thousand years ago with the appearance of Modern Man (Cro-Magnon types), there are not so many disputes about the general character of his natural environment. The real arguments focus on Pliocene times when *Ramapithecus* was extant, and

on the Early Pleistocene times of *Australopithecus.* Although it is generally agreed that the Pliocene witnessed the shrinkage of vast areas of forestland in Africa which may have been replaced by tall grass savannas, there is much less agreement about how man's ancestors adjusted to a gradually changing environment. Did the early hominids come out of the trees, or were they already land dwellers? Did they stay in the woodlands that remained, or did they adopt a predominantly open savanna life? Or did they, as one zoologist has suggested, take to the water, becoming aquatic for a few million years before returning to land living? Only more fossil evidence can help clear up this issue.

But language may not have even begun until much later times than these. If true language only developed in the Upper Paleolithic, for example, then the exact nature of man's habitat at that time is less relevant to his linguistic faculties. By then his tool kit and social activities had already made him less dependent on his environment or on any one particular habitat.

GRADUAL GROWTH OR SUDDEN JUMP

A very hot issue, this one. Was language genesis a natural and normal slow evolutionary development, the inevitable outcome of protohominid adaptations to a changing environment and the result of well-understood evolutionary processes operating on an already existing communicative system similar to those that we now see in apes and other primates? Or was it, on the other hand, an emergent phenomenon, a qualitatively different structural entity appearing at a specific stage of organizational complexity, If the latter—a sudden integrative jump from nonlanguage to language—could it have been a discovery of symboling as described by Helen Keller regarding her mind-bending reorganization of cognitive reality at the water pump; or might it have resulted from a "systemic mutation" of the sort proposed by the biologist Goldschmidt?[1]

This issue is closely related to two others: the relation between language specifically and intellect in general, and the value of comparing man's communicative system with those of other animals. No resolution to the issue is in sight, but a recent review of continuity and discontinuity theories suggests that we should shift our attention from the role of intelligence in phylogenetic history to the ecological context in human evolution, particularly with respect to functions of communication in that context.[2]

SPECIES SPECIFICITY OF LANGUAGE

The question of the evolutionary relationship between capacity to think and capacity to use language can be most profitably posed in terms of Eric Lenneberg's support for the proposal that language is species specific. He is convinced that language abilities are special abilities, distinct and separable from general cognitive abilities that we generally think of as intelligence. Moreover, these language abilities are exclusively possessed by humans; that is, they are specific to the species *Homo sapiens*. At first glance he seems to have a pretty good case. After all, only humans have language, don't they? And isn't it true that although humans vary tremendously in intelligence, even severely retarded humans can learn a language and often manage to use it as grammatically as the next person? There does not appear to be dramatic covariance between intelligence and language capabilities, so they must be distinct from one another.

Lenneberg's case is not so clear-cut as this, however. Nor does he advance such simplistic arguments as these. In support of his contention that language abilities in humans have deep-rooted and specifically linguistic

biological foundations, he points out several lines of evidence.

1. All human societies have language.

2. There are anatomical and physiological correlates of language. These include specialized areas in the brain which have been shown to be associated primarily with speech, special respiratory adjustments for prolonged speech activities, and specialized morphology of the vocal tract. To this contention it has been objected that the correlations are not so exact or complete as one would like, and specifically that direct correlates have not been found to the kinds of phonological and grammatical complexity that distinguishes language from nonlinguistic communication.

3. There is a fixed developmental schedule for the acquisition of language. Language acquisition studies in many societies of the world tend to bear this out. There seems to be a relatively constant onset time which correlates with a child's physical maturation. There is also a relatively regular ordering of other linguistic milestones or stages such as cooing, babbling, holophrastic speech, telegraphic two or three word utterances, etc., which also correlate pretty well with a child's physical maturation. Moreover there is evidence that a critical period for language acquisition exists, after which time language will be learned inadequately if at all, provided that the child has not been exposed to language. To these points it has been objected that we don't know for sure whether this apparently innate scheduling is specific to language or simply a function of more general cognitive development. In fact, Piaget's stages of cognitive development correspond rather nicely with stages of linguistic development.

1. R. Goldschmidt, *The Material Basis of Evolution* (New Haven, Conn.: Yale University Press, 1940).

2. Jane Hill, "Possible Continuity Theories of Language," *Language* 50 (1974):134-50.

But, runs the counterargument, if language reflects general intelligence rather than a special linguistic capacity, then we might expect smart children to learn a language well and stupid ones to do poorly or even fail.

In fact, however, that is exactly what may be happening, even though on a gross level we tend to feel that either you have language or you don't. There simply is no evidence that individuals are equally successful at mastering a linguistic system regardless of intelligence. Clearly there are individual differences in vocabulary size, ability to handle multiple embeddings, ability to define and understand words, ability to reason verbally, and ability to communicate effectively—differences that background and instruction cannot fully explain.

4. It is difficult to prevent humans from learning language. Even with drastic handicaps such as congenital deafness or blindness, children still manage to acquire language. Human children seem to be biologically motivated to speak.

5. Language cannot be taught to nonhumans. This contention is becoming more debatable everyday. Despite the many failures in attempts to teach apes to speak, recent work with chimpanzees has demonstrated some very languagelike abilities in them which some feel are direct evidence of an intellectual capacity for language. As such, this evidence is crucial for our interpretation of how closely language abilities are tied to general intellect. Much of the issue, unfortunately, revolves around what one chooses to call language.

6. No matter how varied the superficial forms of human languages, they all share some universal characteristics of form and substance, and any human being can learn any language. The most obvious characteristics are that, regardless of differing phonemic inventories, all languages employ the phonemic principle, that all languages have words for objects, relations, feelings, and qualities, and that all languages have syntactic rules. It is not at all obvious, however, that analogous formal and substantive universals cannot be found in the behaviors of many vertebrates. Moreover, linguists disagree considerably about what language universals are biologically rooted.

7. With certain types of brain damage, language skills may be lost, leaving other mental skills relatively unaffected. The disease histidinemia, for example, can interfere with language development in children apparently without affecting intelligence. Broca's aphasia is a condition where comprehension of written and spoken speech is normal while speech production is limited and poorly articulated. Another brain condition, Wernicke's aphasia, has symptoms of fluent but contentless speech production along with a lack of ability to understand written and spoken speech. This sort of evidence for special linguistic abilities in humans is equivocal, however, and incompletely understood.

8. There is no good evidence that universal characteristics of current languages have ever been different or smaller in number in recorded history. This argument is very slippery. One might well turn it around and ask for evidence of no change in basic characteristics of language. What, in fact, does it say about the species specificity of language? What it implies is that the things which distinguish language from nonlanguage have been in human languages since their inception, and that language has not evolved since that time. Continuing evolution relates to species specificity indirectly, and can be considered as a separate issue.

CONTINUING EVOLUTION

Is language continuing to evolve? Is it still changing to better equip mankind for his ever-changing natural and social environments? Are man's linguistic-cognitive abilities changing through natural or social selection? Do individual languages increase or decrease in complexity as societies adjust to changing conditions? Once language became established in human populations, did it remain fixed in its fundamental properties and capabilities for information exchange? These questions are part of the continuing evolution issue. And the issue is important; for if language is continuing to change in particular ways, we can then infer that it has changed in the past in these same ways. If it is growing more complex, for example, then we assume that it once was less complex.

To put the issue into focus it must be understood that evolution in a biological sense refers to gradual and continuous changes in the bodily form of living things resulting from interaction with the environment. Language is not a living thing, so we cannot take its evolution literally. Language is not strictly part of man's bodily form either, but it can be viewed metaphorically as an organ or extension that has been very useful for coping with the environment and that has developed a particular form—structure and functions—in response to environmental pressures. This form, however, is actually only symptomatic of underlying neural structure and process in the human brain, and it is the brain itself—among other bodily organs—that has done the evolving. Whether the evolution of the human brain has been specifically directed toward linguistic symptoms or simply toward general intellectual symptoms rendering speech skills possible as a by-product remains the crucially unresolved dispute in the preceding issue.

With the clear understanding that we are dealing with the evolution of language in a metaphorical sense, as before, let me lay out three different positions on continuing linguistic evolution. The first and most widely accepted one is espoused by Joseph Greenberg.[3] Language, as Greenberg sees

it, is not changing in any fundamental ways in response to environmental pressures on social groups. The size of vocabulary is increasing as individual languages increase their vocabularies, but the formal complexity of language remains essentially unchanging. Language change in sound systems and grammatical patterns is constantly going on and will continue to do so, but not in the sense of adaptive radiation, only in the sense of continuing diversification. If sometimes we can see the destruction and rebuilding of systemic patternings, of short-term tendencies toward simplification or increasing complexity in the course of a language's history, in the long run there is no adaptive directionality associated with these changes. Language does not continue to evolve.

The position of Dell Hymes, focusing on the functions of speech with respect to individual communities and their total linguistic resources, is not in direct conflict with that of Greenberg.[4] Rather, he is challenging some of the unstated assumptions and implications of Greenberg's views on continuing evolution. Hymes holds that not all languages are equally well adapted to the needs of their speakers; that languages are not all evolutionarily equivalent; that not all languages have the same range and variety of adjustments to the environment; that community speech habits vary in adaptation and ability to adapt to changing environmental conditions when we view them from a functional perspective; that some languages are evolutionarily more advanced than others in specific ways. Hymes is *not*

3. J. Greenberg, "Language and Evolution," in *Evolution and Anthropology: a Centennial Appraisal,* ed. B. Meggers (Washington, D. C.: Anthropological Society of Washington, 1959), pp. 61-75.

4. D. Hymes, "Functions of Speech: an Evolutionary Approach," in *Anthropology and Education,* ed. F. C. Gruber (Philadelphia: University of Pennsylvania Press, 1961), pp. 55-83.

saying, however, that some languages are "full" languages while others are "primitive." No known languages are primitive in this sense. He is simply arguing that different societies place different emphases on different functions and different components of different speech acts in different kinds of situations, and that these functional differences in linguistic resources can best be understood in a comparative evolutionary context. Languages, in short, continue to evolve.

William Labov claims to favor Greenberg's position, that apart from vocabulary expansion and conceptual development from simple to complex, language change is essentially diversification rather than adaptation.[5] He sees, however, an adaptive function in diversification itself. Diversity, he suggests, may play an adaptive part in cultural pluralism. Diversification in broader perspective may be adaptively providing boundaries that facilitate the organization of social roles within society and that prevent homogeneity by partially isolating breeding populations. Language continues to evolve, sort of.

SUMMARY

This chapter has dealt with a selection of current issues bearing on language genesis. Language must have existed five thousand to ten thousand years ago. It probably originated in the Middle or Upper Paleolithic, but glottogenesis may go back a million years to the earliest times of *Homo erectus*. The scanty evidence available seems to place the homeland of language in the Mediterranean area, possibly in the Near East. Whether all of today's languages have a common ancestor is quite unresolved. I would like to see Swadesh's test for historical retention applied to several other languages before conjecturing on the issue of monogenesis. Bipedalism, tools, and brain development played important and interrelated roles in the evolution of language. How the natural environment interacted with man's changing form and behaviors to promote adaptation through linguistic means is the subject of widely varying opinions. I am personally convinced that language genesis was a natural and normal slow development, but that may simply be because almost any other position would imply that the subject is not worthy of investigation. Some aspects of language seem to be species specific, but the whole issue is opened up by recent research, especially that related to chimpanzees. Languages change, adaptively to some extent. It seems quite possible that further changes in man's brain will lend some directionality to language change, perhaps in the area of structural complexity, possibly in terms of separating linguistic functions.

For Further Reading

Chapple, Elliot *Culture and Biological Man.* New York: Holt, Rinehart and Winston, 1970. This is a fascinating and easy to read view of social interaction in relation to our biological makeup.

Lenneberg, Eric *Biological Foundations of Language.* New York: John C. Wiley & Sons, Inc., 1967. Contains everything you want to know about the title subject and more. Remains a classic, with abundant technical details.

Pilbeam, David *The Ascent of Man.* New York: The Macmillan Co., 1972. An introductory paperback textbook for physical anthropology courses; it makes fossil man come alive.

Washburn, S. L. and Dolhinow, Phyllis J. *Perspectives on Human Evolution One.* New York: Holt, Rinehart and Winston, 1968.

5. W. Labov, *Sociolinguistic Patterns* (Philadelphia: University of Pennsylvania Press, 1972), pp. 324-25.

————. *Perspectives on Human Evolution Two.* New York: Holt, Rinehart and Winston, 1972. This and the preceding constitute a paperback set containing a collection of articles by various authors on the subject of human evolution. The second volume includes six articles on language.

Bibliography

Campbell, Bernard 1966. *Human Evolution.* Chicago: Aldine Publishing Company.

Hill, Jane 1974. "Possible Continuity Theories of Language." *Language* 50:134-50.

Hymes, Dell 1961. "Functions of Speech: an Evolutionary Approach," in *Anthropology and Education,* ed. F. C. Gruber. Philadelphia: University of Pennsylvania Press, pp. 55-83.

Jolly, Alison 1972. *The Evolution of Primate Behavior.* New York: The Macmillan Company.

Lieberman, Philip 1975. *On the Origins of Language.* New York: The Macmillan Company.

Lenneberg, Eric 1969. "On Explaining Language." *Science* 164:635-43.

Morgan, Elaine 1972. *The Descent of Woman.* New York: Stein & Day.

Roe, Anne and Simpson, George Gaylord, eds. 1958. *Behavior and Evolution.* New Haven: Yale University Press.

Simons, Elwyn L. 1972. *Primate Evolution.* New York: The Macmillan Company.

4 | Reconstruction

In this chapter we will take a closer look at linguistic change, directing specific attention to means for reconstructing the past from information presently available. Most methods developed for reconstructing aspects of prior linguistic stages do not carry us very far into the past. The insights that they provide into the workings of linguistic change and language structure are, however, extremely useful for visualizing processes that must have been occurring all along in the evolution of language.

Variation

Looking closely at any speech community, it becomes quite apparent that variation is everywhere. Every individual has his own particular *repertoire* of pronunciations, vocabulary, syntactic rules, and sociolinguistic rules. Specific features of these repertoires are shared to a greater or lesser extent among different members of the community. And everyone's repertoire is continually being modified either by *borrowing* some feature from someone else or by *independently creating* it. The most rapid modification of repertoires occurs during childhood and is usually called learning.

Sometimes a hitherto quite localized feature will spread relatively widely from one personal repertoire to another, traveling along social networks which may or may not be geographically delimited. This spread results in what is termed linguistic change. It may involve a change in pronunciation, a word acquired or lost, or some other shared *innovation* in repertoires. An accumulation of several shared innovations within local groups in the speech community will eventually come to strongly differentiate these groups from one another on the basis of linguistic features, and at some point this will result in different dialects. As intergroup communication becomes more restricted, dialects will become more strongly differentiated—for new innovations are less likely to cross group boundaries—forming a foundation for fissioning along dialect boundary lines to ultimately create mutually unintelligible languages where once there was only one. Frequently we find a whole chain of dialects in which adjacent ones are very similar while the ends of the chain are mutually unintelligible.

Diversification

The formation of languages from dialects, which derive from localized bundles of shared innovations, is referred to as language diversification. Diversification is a process that has been going on in the past, continues in the present, and will persist in the future. Permanent splits in a speech community come about in a variety of ways. A split can result gradually from internal linguistic differentiation of a speech community into groups which slowly come to interact less with each other in terms of frequency and variety of communicative genres. It can come about more rapidly if one portion of a speech community migrates to another location and loses all contact with the original one. It can also be hastened by the intrusion of an alien speech community. Such splitting up or diversification of languages can to some extent be represented diagrammatically as a *family tree*. Every node on the tree represents a language at that point in time. Every node that has had to be postulated from reconstructions of known languages can be termed a *proto-language*. When the linguist constructs a family tree, he divides a group of related languages into subgroups of more closely related languages. Shared phonological, grammatical, lexical, or sociolinguistic features can be used for subgrouping, though they are not all equally useful criteria for showing genetic relationships.

A single innovation or a bundle of communicative features may be borrowed across dialect and language boundaries, spreading outward from a center like ripples in a pond. This is particularly apparent when one speech community gains political, social, or commercial dominance in a larger area and becomes a center of influence, but a similar effect results from any borrowing of linguistic features across language boundaries. The fact that features can spread independently and simultaneously within or between speech communities, and that different speech communities often maintain relatively intense contacts long after they have become separate languages means that family trees are inadequate, if useful, rep-

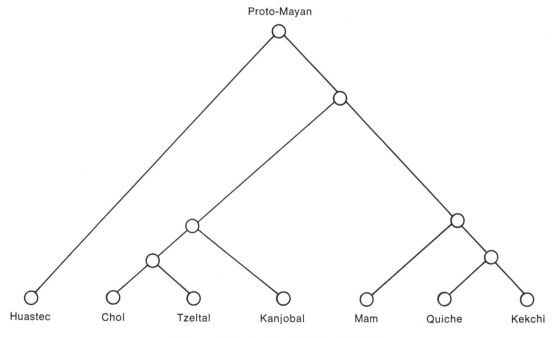

Figure 4.1 MAYAN FAMILY TREE

resentations of language diversification. It also complicates the process of subgrouping by which linguists determine degrees of relationship among languages. Using different features as criteria can apportion the subgroups in different ways.

CHRONOLOGY

If we take several different languages that are related genetically, having a common ancestor language, it is possible to arrange them in subgroups of which the members are more closely related. One way to do this is to compare vocabulary items with essentially the same meaning across languages. Two languages sharing many similar words for the same concepts are more closely related than are languages sharing few, if we exclude borrowed words from the comparisons, and thus are felt to have diverged more recently from a common ancestor. Because borrowing can distort the results of such comparisons, it is best to use areas of vocabulary that are least subject to borrowings or other kinds of change. We can call this the "basic vocabulary."

Morris Swadesh constructed a list of 100 basic vocabulary items including some pronouns, numerals, body parts, kinship terms, and other things likely to be present in every language. This list has been widely used to collect comparable word lists for languages to be subgrouped. Sometimes it is called the Swadesh list, sometimes the lexicostatistics test list, and sometimes the basic vocabulary list. Subgrouping of languages by this method can give a relative chronology of divergences from the common ancestor or protolanguage. And, within limits of statistical error, basic vocabulary can be used to estimate in hundreds of years how long ago at the minimum any two languages have been separated. Lexicostatistical comparisons are used to estimate time depth of lin-

guistic divergence by means of a technique called *glottochronology*.

Glottochronology

Glottochronology begins with the translation of Swadesh's one hundred word basic vocabulary list—which is really a list of meanings—into the two languages to be compared. The next step is to compare each pair of words with the same meaning and try to find a resemblance in form sufficient to match the pair as *cognates*, words that have developed from the same word in a common ancestor language. It is a simple matter then to count the number of cognate pairs that have been identified, out of a possible one hundred. If seventy-four of the pairs are cognates, then the two languages have been separated for at least one thousand years; if thirty-four pairs are cognate, the time depth of separation is two thousand years. A simple formula has been devised, in fact, to give an estimate of time depth for any percentage of cognates, although probabilities of error effectively limit the method to depths of from five hundred to five thousand years. Greater time depths can be reached by applying Swadesh's method to reconstructed forms in two related protolanguages.

Glottochronology as a dating technique hinges on the discovery that basic vocabulary in a language changes at a fairly constant rate on the average. In one thousand years about 14 percent of the forms are replaced by others, about 86 percent are retained. If a parent language splits into two daughter languages which then diverge in isolation from each other, after about one thousand years each of the daughters will have retained about 86 percent of their basic vocabulary in forms that may have been modified by sound change. The 86 percent remaining in one language will not include exactly the same items retained in the other if the daughters developed without mutual contact, so the percentage of cognates they have between them will be 86 percent of 86 percent, which is 74 percent. If the two daughter languages have had partial contact in the intervening years additional agreements will occur so that their shared retention goes above 74 percent, making it look as if they had split up less than one thousand years ago. That is why estimates of divergence are stated in terms of *minimum* centuries; there is always the possibility of some contact since the split.

INTERNAL RECONSTRUCTION

Internal reconstruction in its broader sense refers to any reconstruction of earlier stages of a language or parts of a language from evidence contained within the language, taking no outside language into account. For the most part internal reconstruction focuses on irregularities in a language, holes in a pattern so to speak.

One irregularity in English, for example, is that the morpheme "whelm" seems to occur only in "overwhelm." Because we have such other words as "overawe," "overturn," and "overcome" in which the morphemes following "over" are verbs that occur in other contexts, we might suspect that "whelm" was once a verb root that also had the privilege of occurring in other contexts, and that it dropped out of the language except where it had become fossilized in the word "overwhelm." We could even speculate about its earlier meaning.

Regular sound change tends to irregularize. This is particularly apparent in morphophonemic irregularities, and quite useful for internal reconstruction. Morphophonemic alternations, often found in the juncture areas where affixes meet base forms, are at the real heart of internal reconstruction. An example from Maori, the indigenous language of New Zealand, can illustrate this point well.

MAORI

Active	Gloss	Passive
awhi	"embrace"	awhitia
hopu	"catch"	hopukia
aru	"follow"	arumia
mau	"carry"	mauria
wero	"stab"	werohia

In this example either the passive suffixes are quite variable (*-tia, -kia, -mia,* etc.) or else the single suffix *-ia* causes different consonants to be added to the active base forms before it can be attached to inflect the verb for passive. In either case we see morphophonemic alteration between the consonants *t, k, m,* etc., and $\emptyset$ (zero). A simple synchronic description of this data can be made by postulating the underlying base forms **awhit, *hopuk, *arum, *maur,* and **weroh* (starred to indicate that they don't actually show up in surface representations). To this inventory we must add the underlying base form *-ia* and a single rule that might be stated "consonants go to zero in word-final position." The postulated base forms along with a single morphophonemic rule, then, account for the data synchronically in an elegant way.

What can we infer about an earlier stage of Maori from the morphophonemic alternation exhibited? We can propose that the underlying forms that we had to posit to account synchronically for the data were once surface representations in the active mode, and that at some later point the rule "consonants go to zero in word-final position" was added to the grammar of Maori. In other words, there was a time when this rule did not exist, when consonants did appear at the ends of words, and when our proposed underlying representations reflect the way that active forms of the verbs were pronounced.

Word composition also provides clues about relative ages of words. Analyzable secondary formations such as "arrowhead," "spear-thrower," and "doghouse," are usually assumed to be more recent than single unanalyzable morphemes such as "arrow," "spear," and "dog." We can reconstruct a linguistic stage, then, in which the language had the word "arrow" but no "arrowhead." We also use analyzability as a criterion for reasoning that "South Town" as a place-name is more recent than "Sutton," which in turn was more recent than either of its original components, "south" and "town."

Another kind of internal reconstruction involves words in a language that have been borrowed from other languages. Loanwords have many interesting stories to tell, in fact. Several Tzeltal terms for plants, animals, and political offices, for example, are loans from Spanish. One can infer that the items or social roles designated by these loans are relatively recent introductions to Tzeltal culture, like wheat, horses, pigs, and mayors. An Aztec place-name, Tenango, in the Tzeltal area, gives us a hint about Tzeltal contact with the Aztecs; and a few Spanish cusswords may indicate something about the contexts of Spanish-Tzeltal relations in times gone by. This is cultural information, of course, but nonetheless important to reconstruct. The purely linguistic inferences here are that earlier stages of the langauge did not include the loanwords that can be identified.

Internal reconstruction is both rewarding and somewhat chancy, for many inferences will turn out to be wrong. It can provide interesting hints about previous stages in a language, but these must then be verified with other kinds of evidence. Comparative reconstruction can give us some of that other evidence.

COMPARATIVE RECONSTRUCTION

Comparative reconstruction makes use of more than one language in order to arrive at conclusions about earlier linguistic stages. Central to this kind of reconstruction is the Comparative Method which has evolved from a century of philological work as a set of principles for making linguistic inferences and as a series of steps to be applied in the analysis of linguistic data. What makes it profitable is the interesting fact that much sound change is regular and occurs for the most part in particular phonological environments.

As an instance of regular sound change we can look at the Latin k as in /klarus/, /kervus/, and /kawsa/, which developed into three different reflexes in modern French: /kler/ "clear," /serf/ "stag," and /šoz/ "thing," respectively. The Latin k's that had preceded an o or were in a consonant cluster remained k's in French, before front vowels like e and i Latin k changed to an s, and before an a it became š in French. We could look at many more Latin words with k and predict from their environments with complete certainty which k's will show up in French words as k, which will come out s, and which ones will become š. This is regular sound change.

Jakob Grimm noticed the effects of regular sound change quite early, and in 1819 published a volume of sound correspondences between Germanic and other Indo-European languages. Notice, for example, the initial consonants in Latin frater, Russian brat, French frère, Sanskrit bharta, and German bruder all of which mean 'brother'. The Latin f corresponds to a Russian b, a French f, a Sanskrit bh, a German b, and an English b in this position. There are many many more sets of cognate words in these languages which exhibit the same sound correspondences—the result of regular sound change. Not all sound change is absolutely regular, so there will be exceptions in occasional correspondence sets, but there is enough regularity to make the comparative method very useful for reconstructing words and sound systems of earlier protolanguages.

The five essential steps to the comparative method can be understood best in terms of an illustration like the following, in which we have short word lists from three different Mayan languages.

Step 1 consists of assembling apparent cognates from the languages that are being compared, throwing all borrowed words out of consideration from the outset. Step one was accomplished by arranging the data below. The words *be : p'e :* and *be* from row 2 are an example of a *cognate set;* they look alike and have the same meaning, so we can be pretty sure that they reflect the same word in an earlier ancestor of the three languages.

TZELTAL	TOJOLABAL	TZOTZIL	
1 ak'	aᵖ	ok'	"give"
2 be	p'e	be	"road"
3 ič'	iᵖ	ič'	"hold"
4 uč'	uᵖ	uč'	"drink"
5 bak	p'ak	bok	"bone"
6 k'abal	k'ap'al	k'obol	"hand"
7 pim	pim	pim	"thick"

Step 2 involves uncovering the systematic sound correspondences that link the cognate sets. In doing so we establish (sound) *correspondence sets* like the following: from row 1 there are $a:a:o$ and $k':^ʔ:k'$; from row 2 there are $b:p':b$ and $e:e:e$; and so on.

Step 3 is taken when we posit some protosound to underlie each correspondence set. Sometimes this is simple as with the *e*'s, *i*'s, *u*'s, *k*'s, *m*'s, and *l*'s. An *i* in one language corresponds to an *i* in the other two, for example, so we posit an $*i$ as the protosound. For the correspondence set $b:p':b$ we have to decide between b and p' to rep-

resent the protosound. For lack of any reasons not to do so, we can let the majority rule here and opt for $*b$ as the protosegment. A similar decision gives us $*a$ for the set $a:a:o$.

Then there is the seemingly contradictory pair of correspondence sets $k':k':k'$ and $k':^ʔ:k'$ which we must reconcile by looking for an environmental difference between them. It can be found in the word-final positioning of the set $k':^ʔ:k'$. Word-final and non-word-final position are different environments: one correspondence set appears in one of these environments only, and the other appears only in the other environment. So here we must specify a rule for predicting which correspondence set will apply in a particular situation; in word-final position $k':^ʔ:k'$ will apply, the other set $k':k':k'$ will apply elsewhere. Because k' occurs even in Tojolabal in initial position, it is likely that it once occurred in final position too in Tojolabal as it still does in Tzeltal and Tzotzil. Therefore we reconstruct a protosegment $*k'$ and the simple rule $*k'$ in final position changed to ^{ʔ} in Tojolabal, remaining as a k' in other positions. It looks like additional data would show a $c':č':č'$ to go along with $č':^ʔ:č'$, so we can posit a $*č$ in analogy to $*k'$ that behaved in the course of time just as $*k'$ did, going to ^{ʔ} in Tojolabal when in final position. Now we have reconstructed a protosound to stand for, and rules to account for, every correspondence set in the data.

Step 4 is to reconstruct words in the protolanguage from cognate sets in the daughter languages by using our reconstructed protosounds. This gives us the protowords $*ak'$, $*be$, $*ič'$, $*uč'$, $*bak$, $*k'abal$, and $*pim$, as well as the meanings "give," "road," "hold," "drink," "bone," "hand," and "thick," respectively. The reconstructed forms just happen to look just like the Tzeltal forms, so we need no sound change rules to account here for the evolution of Tzeltal from the protolanguage. Very often, however, none of the daughter languages mirror the protolanguage in this way.

Step 5 consists of stating rules for the sound changes that have occurred in the development of each daughter language. In this case we need rules only for Tzotzil and Tojolabal. Tzotzil needs only one rule: all $*a$'s go to o. Tojolabal needs two: (1) $*k^!$ and $*č^!$ in final position go to $^?$, elsewhere they remain the same and (2) b goes to $p^!$. All such rules should be reasonable, involving changes that have been known to occur in other languages.

The reconstruction is now complete. We have, by showing regular sound correspondences, demonstrated that the three languages are genetically related; and we have partially reconstructed the protolanguage. It should be noted that the comparative method demonstrated here allows us to reconstruct morphology and semantics as well as sound systems. Syntax can be reconstructed as well, using variations and refinements of this theme.

Comparative reconstruction can give much more than purely linguistic information. If we can reconstruct some plant and animal terms, for example, we may well get clues about the environment in which the protolanguage speakers lived. We can use reconstructed kinship terms and meanings to learn something of social organization in the community of protolanguage speakers, and a variety of other information also becomes accessible.

Additionally, we can appeal to *migration theory*, elaborated from ideas of Edward Sapir, for help in determining the aboriginal homeland of the protolanguage. In its simplest form, migration theory takes into account the geographical distribution and degrees of differentiation of all daughter languages to propose a homeland area that involves the smallest number of independent migrations that could result in the present situation.

Comparative reconstruction has several different techniques at its disposal, as we have seen. Rarely have they been used to carry us earlier than about seven thousand years ago. Even in that span, much information gets swept away in the tides of time. Recently, however, techniques have been proposed to delve even earlier, perhaps to the genesis of language. Let's take a look at three of them.

PHONETIC SYMBOLISM, ROOT MORPHEMES, AND SUBMERGED SEMANTIC FEATURES

As with the traditional comparative method, the three approaches to be mentioned here are concerned with the relation between sound and meaning. They differ somewhat in holding different aspects of this relationship constant, and to some extent in their ultimate aims.

Consider first the following series of words: glitter, glimmer, glow, glisten, and glare. They all share an essential meaning that includes the notion of light, and they all share an initial *gl* sound. One might propose that they incorporate a "fossilized" morpheme *gl* within them. By holding the form constant we can look for a shared global meaning on the assumption that at one time *gl* was a separate morpheme in our language which has since become fossilized in some words while the free morpheme representation itself was lost.

Consider next the pairs: here, there; near, far; this, that; and me, you. Each pair includes an alternation between a higher more front vowel and a lower more back vowel. And the higher more front vowel in each case is in the member of the pair that refers to something closer to the speaker. Distance from speaker seems to be indicated here by vowel quality. Even more interesting, many languages incorporate the same distinctions in vowel quality in precisely the same way in their own words for these pairs.

Morris Swadesh

Swadesh, referred to earlier, used both these kinds of relationships between sound and meaning to reconstruct aspects of the "first" language. What he was looking for was, for the most part, nonarbitrary connections between linguistic forms and human thought processes (i.e., meaning), or natural *sound symbolism*. He found grammatical sound symbolism in the widespread usage among the world's peoples of internal vowel alternation and reduplication for inflecting words in terms of proximity to speaker, shape, intensity, repetition, and other qualities, and then he carried these notions backwards in time. He also found that certain consonants (e.g., *p, t, k, m, n, ʔ*) commonly occurred in words that could be ultimately related to the imitation of sounds occurring as the results of actions. Swadesh believed that the sound symbolic alternations and imitations he found in today's languages and in reconstructed protolanguages were utilized more fully in primordial times, and that their symbolic nature made them productive in languages throughout the history of language diversification; in other words they have existed as small pockets of self-correcting tendencies functioning somewhat to counteract the other normal linguistic process of divergence.

Mary Foster

Another linguist, Mary Foster, has been more traditional in her approach but just about as daring in the scope of her attempts to reconstruct a primordial language. Not interested in symbolism as such, she sees the form as primary and seeks to relate mean-

ing to it. She has proposed ten working assumptions and criteria of comparison which she calls postulates. Perhaps the best illustration of her approach can be found in the following paraphrases of three postulates.

1. Primordial morphemes are rarely lost from a language because they are transmitted to a variety of lexical items.

2. Reconstructions must be based on whole vocabularies or on very large reconstructed vocabularies so that the primordial morphemes dispersed in the lexicon can be identified and recovered.

3. Roots that appear unanalyzable in daughter languages represent earlier morpheme sequences that have become fossilized.

One goal, then, is to reconstruct the shape of every primordial morpheme and to pair it with a meaning. Foster's work is more rigorous than that of Swadesh but has led to some similar conclusions about the earliest stages of language and has generated some exciting proposals about Proto-Indo-European.

One conclusion she has reached is that the primordial language had as few as sixteen meaning-bearing units, each of which was both a phoneme and a morpheme. In other words, each morpheme was represented by a single phoneme, and there may have been only sixteen of them at first. At some later point a string of these meaning-bearing phonemes came to be conceptualized by the speakers in terms of a single semantic component and the stem became frozen in the language with its new meaning: for example, when **fkr* came to have the unitary meaning "circle" instead of the complex additive meaning "elongation of a physical unit in the direction of becoming reunited."

Marshall Durbin

A third linguist, Durbin has been working with submerged semantic features expressed as sound alternations. His semantic features are rather different in kind from most of those dealt with by Foster and Swadesh. Where their reconstructions deal very largely with spatio-temporal relationships and actions, his identifications are of such concepts as ownership and possession. Durbin, it must be said, is not explicitly trying to reconstruct earlier stages of human language, nor even of Yucatec in which the alternations referred to occur.

Look over the following Yucatec examples in which each member of a pair differs from the other only by a single sound; each has either ʔ or *w*.

1. ʔin ʔeʔel "my egg" (laid by my hen, POSSESSION)
   ʔin weʔel "my testicle" (on my own body, OWNERSHIP)
2. ʔin ʔookol "my thief" (he who steals from me, POSSESSION)
   ʔin wookol "my robbery" (what I steal, OWNERSHIP)
3. ʔin ʔaktaan "my leader" (he who leads me, POSSESSION)
   ʔin waktaan "my follower" (he whom I lead, OWNERSHIP)

For many years students of Yucatec were unaware that the same semantic distinctions lay submerged in the phonological distinctions between members of all these pairs and others. In these examples, the ʔ*in* beginning each word is the Yucatec inflection for first person singular possessive of nouns. The rest of the word is the stem, consisting of a noun root prefixed by one or the other of two alternants, ʔ or *w*, which are phonologically conditioned alternants in several other Mayan languages, but not here. Ordinarily we would think that the first person singular inflection is the possessor of the thing denoted by the following stem. The problem here is that the meaning of the stem is variable and depends on the rela-

tionship between phonological alternants and person prefix.

Many languages make grammatical distinctions between things that are *inalienable* (ownership) or not really capable of being given away, such as body parts or relatives, and things which are *alienable* (possession) or capable of being given away. Yucatec seems to be marking this distinction between alienable and inalienable with a simple sound alternation and extending the conceptual distinction productively to create different meanings of words that may at one time have had only a single meaning.

Semantic features such as possession, ownership, and many others are sometimes subtly submerged in linguistic form, as these are. Fifty years ago, Edward Sapir suggested that submerged features might be very useful in making comparisons and helping to establish genetic relationships among languages that have been separated so long that their superficial structures are very different. If, on close inspection, some such semantic features show up in one way or another in all the world's languages, then we might expect that similar conceptual distinctions were made in languages of the distant past, regardless of whether they illustrate common genetic relationship or simply common psychological processes.

TYPOLOGY

Around the turn of the century and earlier, linguistic researchers were preoccupied with the formulation of linguistic typologies. According to several different kinds of criteria, but especially word formation, they would lump the then known languages of the world into different categories. One nineteenth-century typology distinguished three kinds of languages, based on the degree of cohesiveness between meaningful elements in words. The three categories were (1) *isolating* languages, like Chinese, which consist simply of invariable word roots having no morphology that are strung together in strict order to create sentences; (2) *agglutinating* languages, like Turkish, in which prefixes and suffixes are mechanically tacked onto roots without change to modify their meanings; and (3) *inflectional* languages, like Latin, where internal changes in words go along with meaning modification. Some early scholars proposed that these types in the order given here reflected a sequence from simple to complex in the evolution of language.

Problems arise with this interpretation, however. There are actually no existing languages representing these types in pure form. Moreover, there seems to be a cyclic rather than an evolutionary development in historical stages of these languages. For example, Chinese and English are both predominantly isolating now, but in earlier times—English until quite recently—they were primarily inflectional, and both give indications of becoming more agglutinating in the future. This, of course, does not really destroy the hypothesis that pure types, not represented by living languages, reflect an evolutionary sequence. It simply does not substantiate it.

Sapir proposed a more encompassing formulation of typological criteria early in this century, and others have developed independent typologies more recently, but rarely nowadays are any of these projected in evolutionary terms. With the abandonment of ethnocentric prejudices, it may be fruitful in the future to reexamine the potential of typological schemes for reflecting developmental trends, particularly in view of the progress being made in understanding language universals.

SUMMARY

Linguistic and cultural reconstruction starting from present-day languages has been going on for a long time in linguistics and anthropology. The more traditional methods of reconstruction have been slowly increasing our knowledge of prehistoric languages, but the farther back we push, the more speculative the reconstructions become. A conservative limit on traditional techniques might be about seven thousand years into the past. Bold and recently reconsidered methods, including sound symbolism, root morphemes, and submerged semantic features have been proposed to reach back further in time for a handhold on early stages of language. Typologies based on grammatical processes found in present-day languages and projected diachronically have been out of fashion for some time now, but our increasing linguistic sophistication and continuing inquiry into language universals may bring about future speculation along these lines.

For Further Reading

Anttila, Raimo *An Introduction to Historical and Comparative Linguistics.* New York: The Macmillan Company, 1972. A comprehensive introductory source on language change and on methods of comparative and internal reconstruction; highly condensed.

Gudschinsky, Sarah "The ABCs of Lexicostatistics (Glottochronology)." *Word* 12 (1956): 175-210. This article contains detailed instructions and explanations for those interested in applying the technique of glottochronology.

Sapir, Edward *Language.* New York: Harcourt, Brace & World, 1921. Now reprinted as a Harvest paperback, this book contains a clear discussion of language typologies on pages 57-146. The rest of the book is an insightful and lucid exposition on language in general.

Bibliography

Haas, Mary R. 1969. *The Prehistory of Languages.* The Hague: Mouton and Co., Publishers.

Hoenigswald, Henry M. 1960. *Language Change and Linguistic Reconstruction*. Chicago: The University of Chicago Press.

Hymes, Dell 1960. "Lexicostatistics so Far." *Current Anthropology* 1:4-44.

King, Robert D. 1969. *Historical Linguistics and Generative Grammar*. Englewood Cliffs, New Jersey: Prentice-Hall, Inc.

Langacker, Ronald W. 1973. *Language and its Structure*, 2d ed. New York: Harcourt Brace Jovanovich, Inc.

Lehmann, Winfred P. 1962. *Historical Linguistics: An Introduction*. New York: Holt, Rinehart and Winston.

Mandelbaum, David G., ed. 1958. *Selected Writings of Edward Sapir*. Berkeley and Los Angeles: University of California Press.

Swadesh, Morris 1951. "Diffusional Cumulation and Archaic Residue as Historical Explanations." *Southwestern Journal of Anthropology* 7:1-21.

——— 1959. "Linguistics as an Instrument of Prehistory." *Southwestern Journal of Anthropology* 15:20-35.

5 | Origins

In the preceding chapters we have seen many avenues of inquiry into the perplexing puzzle of language origins. Chimpanzees, fossil man, and the brain have all been mentioned. Recent research in each of these areas has led to particularly significant advances in our understanding and has interesting implications for glottogenesis, so I want to take up each topic in turn and with a bit more detail.

ANIMAL COMMUNICATION SYSTEMS

There is considerable disagreement over just how much we can learn about human communication from studying nonhumans. What can bird songs, honeybee dancing, cricket chirping, dog barking, or monkey grunting tell us about the development of our own speech, you might ask. Quite a bit, actually. To study these systems requires attention to details, factors, and functions that can easily be overlooked in human speech because it is so familiar. In the second place, the evolutionary process itself guarantees that some aspects of our communicative system will be shared with other animals, since speciation proceeds adaptively and species survival necessitates some means of information transfer. Third, our closest relatives in the phylogenetic scale are likely to share many communicative characteristics with humans. If we let these evolutionary relatives represent our own more direct ancestors, then differences between the two systems of communication become things that need explanation in hypotheses about how the gap between linguistic and prelinguistic communication was bridged. These differences must be explained in terms of adaptive superiority in the particular ecological contexts in which protolinguistic hominids evolved. Before zeroing in on our closest relatives, the chimpanzees, let us start with some of the characteristics possessed by all human languages.

Design Features

Charles Hockett, mentioned earlier with reference to his theory of "blending," has isolated sixteen "design features" that can be either present or absent in any communication system, all of which are present in human speech and some of which occur in communication systems of other animals. They are the following:

1. Vocal Auditory Channel. Many other animals depend, of course, on other communicative channels. Two adaptive advantages for language of using an auditory perceptual mode and vocal production are that

54

very little body energy is required to generate messages, and that most of the body is left free for other activities conducted simultaneously.

2. Broadcast Transmission and Directional Reception. While our speech travels in all directions at once, we can usually distinguish the direction that a spoken message is coming from. There is an obvious adaptive value to locating the sources of sounds, spoken or otherwise.

3. Rapid Fading. Unlike animal tracks and most chemically perceived messages, speech signals immediately fade away, leaving the system free for new messages.

4. Interchangeability. Unlike the mating displays of crickets, spiders, and other animals, speech signals can be transmitted or received interchangeably by adult members of any speech community.

5. Complete Feedback. A human speaker hears everything he says and can therefore, to some extent, perceive himself as others do. This certainly has an important effect on learning, making it faster and easier.

6. Specialization. The production of speech signals presumably serves no direct biological function. This contrasts with the panting sounds made by a hot dog. The dog's panting is biologically necessary to keep him at the right body temperature and only incidentally generates any information bearing signals.

7. Semanticity. Speech signals can refer to features in the speaker's external environment. Language, in this sense, is meaningful.

8. Arbitrariness. Most speech signals share no characteristics of sound or form with the objects or events that they refer to. The relationship is essentially arbitrary, depending on symbols rather than icons. This is not to say that no linguistic forms are iconic, just that many aren't.

9. Discreteness. Most of the elementary signalling units of speech make absolute distinctions of meaning: for example, the range of possible pronunciations between what is heard as a *p* and what is heard as a *b* make no referentially meaningful differences. The vocal repertoires of many animals show continuous gradations between forms which correspond to graded meanings, in the same way that we can convey degrees of anger by corresponding degrees of loudness. The distinction between discrete and continuous is that between digital and analog communication.

10. Displacement. Linguistic messages may be displaced in space or time, referring to things outside of the perceptual field of the communicators. Can you imagine a chimpanzee referring to an event of last year or to the temperature of Venus? Perhaps not, but a chimp can refer to things that are considerably outside of its perceptual field.

11. Openness. Sometimes called productivity, this feature means that new messages can be coined easily and can be immediately understood in context. We now know that the chimpanzee can generate new messages, and even with a digital gestural system. One chimp, for example, invented the name for "duck" by combining already acquired signs for "water" and "bird," and gesturally labeled a watermelon "fruit-drink."

12. Tradition. Linguistic conventions can be passed on from one generation to another outside of the germ plasm. From genetic to cultural transmission of traits is simply one long continuum, however, when you think about it.

13. Duality of Patterning. A most difficult concept, this means that meaningless signal elements in a communicative system are combined, *and recombined,* in patterned ways to produce meaningful messages. Notes in some bird songs and phonemes in language behave in this manner. The fact that words and sentences also combine and recombine hierarchically has led some to suggest that this design feature should be changed to "multiplicity of patterning."

14. Prevarication. Linguistic messages can be false, misleading, or deliberately meaningless. "Playing possum" and other ruses carried out by some birds and mammals seem to represent analogous behavior.

15. Reflexiveness. This design feature refers to the ability to communicate about the communication system itself. Most observers claim that this is unique to man, but observations of primate behavior show that there are many metamessages generated, particularly in play: messages, for example, suggesting such meanings as "Don't take my attack seriously, I'm only playing."

16. Learnability. A human speaker can learn another language. There can be no doubt that many other animals can at least learn new signals and their meanings, and that many make prodigious imitators. Chimpanzees have shown the most clear-cut abilities to learn new communication systems.

When Hockett proposed the first thirteen of these design features in 1960, he treated them as all-or-nothing features.[1] Any given animal communication system either possessed a feature or it didn't. Furthermore he suggested that the evolution of land mammals, from elephants to man, involved the more or less sequential acquisition from the first to the thirteenth of these design features in their communication systems, and that only man has displacement, productivity, and duality of patterning. The problem, as he saw it at that time, was to propose reasonable ways of introducing duality, productivity, and displacement into a primate communication system that supposedly lacked these features. Blending was one of his solutions.

Since 1960 it has become abundantly clear that most—and perhaps all—of Hockett's design features are not all-or-nothing propositions. There are degrees of semanticity, degrees of arbitrariness, of displacement, openness, prevarication, reflexiveness, and so on. There are even degrees of discreteness and duality.

Moreover, within human communication systems we find surviving subsystems or encapsulations such as gesture, interjections, paralinguistic phenomena, touch, and glossolalia which do not fully meet the design feature criteria in the way that language does. These nonlinguistic encapsulations must at one time have carried a greater share of the communicative load in hominid societies.

These considerations make the problem of going from prelanguage to language in terms of design features much more accessible for solution in some ways. But to do so, we now have to find out for sure how much of each feature is present in chimpanzee communication under natural circumstances. We also want to know how close to human language a chimpanzee is capable of coming. In other words we have to study both normal communicative performance in wild chimpanzees and their capacity for communicative performance under optimal learning conditions. Some very exciting things are being discovered in both of these areas at the present time.

The Untrained Chimpanzee

Until comparatively recently, chimpanzee behavior in the wild state has remained largely mysterious. We didn't know before, for example, that some chimpanzee bands kill and eat smaller animals, or that they exhibit elaborate sharing behavior with meat and other kinds of food involving a complex of relatively specific gestures, or that they use and make primitive tools, or that they have excellent memories. And we are still quite ignorant about the details of their communication system. Nevertheless, some important general facts about chim-

1. Charles F. Hockett, "The Origin of Speech," *Scientific American* 203 (1960):89-96.

panzee social life and communication have been observed, many of which are similar to what we know about other primates.

Chimpanzee communicative signals are whole complexes of behavior involving facial expression, posture, movement, and often sound. By itself, a facial expression, a gesture, or a vocalization would usually be an incomplete signal, although some parts of a signal may vary independently to express level of involvement, seriousness of purpose, or some other graded aspect of meaning in a manner analogous to our use of paralinguistic voice qualities for expressive meaning. The visual channel is primary in chimpanzee communication, auditory cues functioning to catch the visual attention of a receiver or to modify meanings conveyed through the channels of sight, touch, and smell.

Context is of overwhelming importance to the interpretation of chimpanzee communicative acts. The same behavioral constellation constituting a particular signal means quite different things in different contexts. Its interpretation depends upon the social situation and immediate surrounding environment as well as on directly preceding events. Because chimpanzees live in social groups in which members have more or less continuous and long-term contact with one another, contextual information is pretty much common information, and each member gets to know the idiosyncratic habits and behavior patterns of the others rather well. In similar situations, humans also seem to be able to get along together and interact with a minimum of creative verbalization. Common understandings based on extensive shared experiences allow a small homogeneous group to function with a very limited overt communication system.

Although environmental information can be inferred from chimpanzee signalling, they communicate almost nothing explicit about their physical environments, most messages

displaying their emotional states. Nonetheless, primarily expressive signals of chimps have been noticed that seem to function as embryonic greetings, rejections, offers, threats, requests, attention getting devices, challenges, reprimands, warnings, lies, and even something like pointing or naming.

To sum it up, although chimpanzee communication is predominantly expressive and visual-gestural, whereas human language is particularly elaborated for referential and vocal auditory messages, if we look at communicative functions, the distance between the two systems seems shorter than might otherwise be expected. But this is only half the story. Chimpanzees have recently been found to have previously unguessed at capacities for languagelike communication.

The Trained Chimpanzee

Many unsuccessful attempts have been made in the last fifty years to teach chimpanzees to speak. One such attempt was initiated in 1947 by a couple of psychologists, Keith and Catherine Hayes, who adopted Viki, a young chimpanzee, into their childless household. By the time of Viki's death, almost seven years later, she had learned to say only seven words, and not too clearly at that. She had also demonstrated in a battery of tests, however, a surprising ability to solve problems, formulate new concepts, remember things for long periods of time, imitate human activities, and communicate her desires through gesture.

And then, along came Washoe the chimpanzee in 1966—the first real breakthrough in two-way communication between human and chimpanzee. Washoe was taught to communicate in American Sign Language, a system of manually produced visual symbols—analogous to words in speech—which are composed of individually meaningless signal elements. Under the direction of Beatrice and R. Allen Gardner, Washoe learned sign language in stages unmistakably like those of a human child learning to speak. The meanings of signs were generalized to classes of referents, signs were put together in increasingly longer combinations, and there was an increase in the variety of semantic relations expressed by sign combinations. By the end of three years Washoe had acquired 132 signs of American Sign Language, and was using them productively and possibly with an elementary syntax. She was signing such requests as "go in," "tickle Washoe," and "open blanket" as well as descriptions like "drink red." Perhaps her "Washoe sorry" could be considered an apology. Washoe could name objects, and upon seeing herself in a full length mirror, was able to name herself. She did, however, ask very few questions.

At about the same time that Washoe was learning sign language, another chimpanzee, Sarah, was being trained in California to manipulate plastic symbols of various shapes and colors representing words like "prefer," "milk," "Mary," "all," "none," "name of," "yes," and "blue." David Premack, a psychologist who designed Sarah's rigorous training program, introduced her by steps to the construction of plastic token sentences. Sarah was carefully trained to use tokens standing for negation, questions, the if/then relation, and other grammatical concepts, and at one point she was able to respond appropriately to a sentence instructing her to "put the banana in the pail and the apple in the dish." She could name and describe things when asked, and clearly distinguished agent from recipient in terms of word order. So far, Sarah's training program has not called for her to ask questions.

At Yerkes Primate Research Center in Georgia, another chimpanzee named Lana has been taught to communicate by punching computer keys, in a specially devised token symbol "language" called Yerkish. Within eighteen months from the start of her training Lana was able to produce new and grammatically correct word strings in Yerkish. She also began to ask for the names of things and subsequently to use the new names in sentences requesting the things themselves.

At least six other chimpanzees are currently under study, and the Gardners have begun a new project in which chimpanzees acquired from birth are being reared by people who are fluent in American sign language. The next few years should produce many new insights into the communicative abilities of *Pan troglodytes*, our closest living relatives, but the evidence already seems to indicate that most of the intellectual and communicative differences between apes and man are differences in degree rather than in kind, except that the visual channel is primary in apes, whereas man's higher linguistic functions make use of auditory coding. Did speech develop out of an already elaborated gesture system not wholly instinctive in nature?

THE HUMAN BRAIN

Looking down on a brain from the outside may conjure up images of a walnut split down the middle into two deeply fissured halves that are linked together deep in the central area. The exterior portion of these halves consists of tissue layers called *cortex* covering the two cerebral hemispheres. It is the size and elaboration of the *cerebrum* that most obviously distinguishes man from his closest primate relatives, and it is here in the cerebral cortex that the highest integration and organization of the nervous system including the senses is achieved. In man one cerebral hemisphere is dominant, usually the left one, and is functionally associated with speech and hearing as well as other analytical tasks, such as mathematics. The other hemisphere is more closely associated with synthesis of ideas, aesthetic appreciation of music and art, and with spatial relations. The left hemisphere has direct sensory input from and motor control over the right side of the body, and the opposite obtains for the right hemisphere. They share information through a large connecting bundle of nerve fibers, the *corpus callosum*. If you cut this link between the cerebral hemispheres, as in "split-brain" patients, subtle behavioral differences result. Split-brain patients, for example, seem not to lose many skills requiring coordination of both hands, but learn new ones only with considerable difficulty. Information exchanged between hemispheres must be stored separately in both it would seem.

The two hemispheres are also connected with the *brain stem* which is essentially an enlargement at the end of the spinal cord. Surrounding the brain stem and enclosed by the cerebral hemispheres are a number of structures—including the thalamus, hypo-thalamus, and hippocampus—which together constitute much of the *limbic system*, regulating our emotions and associated with emotion laden speech vocalizations.

Attached to the brain stem in front is a tiny gland, the *pituitary*, that secretes hormones influencing our growth and maturation; projecting to the rear is the *cerebellum*, which regulates and coordinates complex muscular movements but does not initiate them.

Two kinds of cells are present in the brain: *neurons*, some 100 billion of them, and ten times as many *glia*, which are packed between the neurons. For years, the glia have been thought only to perform chemical housekeeping tasks in caring for neurons, but they may also be involved in the protein synthesis that is currently believed to underlie learning and memory. Neurons are interconnected by fine branching tentacles forming the nerve network, and in the miniscule gaps between tentacles of one neuron

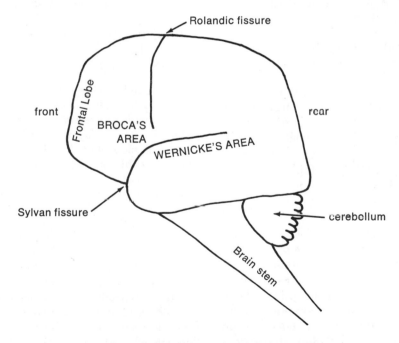

Figure 5.1 LEFT SIDE VIEW OF THE BRAIN

Evolutionary Changes in the Brain

The brain has changed during the course of hominid evolution in several ways. Most obvious have been a tremendous enlargement of the cerebral hemispheres, particularly in front, an increase in the number and depth of convolutions in the cerebral cortex along with more cortex, and an increase in the cross-sectional area of the corpus callosum. In addition there has been an increase in the number of brain cells, the growth of new areas of cortex, an increase in the length and quantity of branching nerve tentacles, and a decrease in cell density of the cortex. Moreover the brain has become *lateralized*, having a dominant and slightly larger left hemisphere, which is functionally distinct from the right, or minor, hemisphere.

Our enlarged frontal lobes of the cerebrum are poorly understood, but they seem to be related to achievement motivation and to inhibitory circuits, keeping our emotions under control among other things. Elaboration of the cerebral cortex, particularly in the evolutionarily late "association" areas, can be related to development and integration of sensory modalities (such as vision, hearing, and touch) and to a need for complex interconnections among different areas of the cortex as well as between cortical areas and the limbic system. Control and integration appear to be the key concepts here. Control of—and consequent distancing from—direct emotional type-responses to situations would clearly have adaptive advantages, facilitating selective attention to environmental stimuli as well as selective and appropriate responses. Reasoned reactions are often superior to emotional ones. Integration of the sensory modes allows learning and memory associated with one modality to be transferred to others. Development of the corpus callosum is relatable to increased information transfer between the hemispheres, broadly linking our analytic and synthetic abilities which are at least partially localized by hemisphere as we have learned from split-brain experiments.

Lateralization of the brain, a most notable consequence of the evolutionary process, is manifested in the asymmetry of cerebral hemispheres. Language functions are attributed primarily to the dominant hemisphere. Lateralization also shows up as preference for one hand or the other, usually the right hand. Hand preferences can be observed in individual apes too, but it seems to be only an individual rather than a species phenomenon.

Two Speech Systems

It has been suggested that human speech involves two different systems, one *limbic* and one *neocortical:*

The first and phylogenetically older system is located in the limbic system, is bilaterally represented without hemispheric dominance, antedates primate development, is closely related to emotional, motivational, and autonomic factors, and is capable of transmitting only signals of low informational content. The second system is supplementary to the first, was developed in man, is neocortical, lateralized, and usually dominant in the left hemisphere. As is so often true in the central nervous system, it did not arise "from" or "out of" the old system but from new tissue, namely the neocortical association areas. This new tissue permitted speech greater independence from emotional factors and provided it thereby the means and circuitry to carry compact, dense, and precise informational loads. This system arose in parallel with the old, surpassed it, and relegated the old system to a subordinate role.[2]

Electrical stimulation of limbic areas in both monkeys and humans produces similar results; crude, emotional vocalizations are elicited involuntarily. Such sounds come out in humans even when an important area for nonlimbic speech production has been destroyed. Apparently the two speech systems are interdependent—neocortical speech predominating in symbolic referential usage of language. But in times of emotional stress the limbic system can reassert its evolutionary precedence, producing such semi- or non-voluntary expressive speech as exclamations, expletives, or gibberish.

Two Brains

The limbic speech system in man—and the analogous communicative system in other primates—is not lateralized. But man, while evolving new areas of cortex, particularly apparent in the left hemisphere, has developed another speech system, a semiautonomous system useful in rational discourse. There are several lines of evidence to indicate that language is at least partly localized in the left hemisphere of most humans.

Early examinations of patients with speech disturbances due to brain damage led to the discovery that damage in particular areas could cause more or less predictable kinds of language problems. One set of symptoms, called Broca's aphasia, consisted primarily of problems in speech production. The patient spoke little, only with great effort, and then with poor pronunciation. Moreover he would omit grammatical function words, and he would write about as poorly as he spoke. Yet such a patient might understand the speech of others quite well, and be able to sing a melody perfectly. Often a patient with Broca's aphasia would have brain damage in the frontal lobe of the left hemisphere in an area called Broca's area.

Another set of symptoms, called Wernicke's aphasia, was quite different, consisting mostly of problems in speech comprehension. The patient could and would speak quickly and easily, sounding quite normal—except that the speech would contain very little information, being filled with repetitions, fillers, circumlocutions leading nowhere, and frequently inappropriate words. The patient would also display an inability to understand the speech of others. Often such a patient would be found to have lesions in the left temporal lobe of his brain, near where the left ear is located, in what is now called Wernicke's area. Another speech area is located.

A third area of the brain, called the motor speech area because it participates in controlling outgoing nerve impulses directing the articulation of sounds, is not so directly relevant to language organization in the brain. It, too, has been seen to cause speech disturbances and often paralysis of the opposite side of the body when damaged.

Electrical stimulation of various points on the cerebral cortex largely confirmed the presence of general speech areas in the dominant hemisphere. More recent work involving patients whose hemispheres have been surgically separated—split-brain patients—has begun to clarify some of the more important differences between hemispheres.

To put it dramatically, split-brain patients have two separate and autonomous brains. With such people it is possible to present visual stimuli independently to each hemisphere. It turns out that the right hemi-

2. Bryan W. Robinson, "Anatomical and Physiological Contrasts Between Human and Other Primate Vocalizations," in *Perspectives on Human Evolution 2*, eds. S. L. Washburn and Phyllis Dolhinow (New York: Holt, Rinehart and Winston, 1972), p. 442.

sphere is mute. Presented with a picture of a banana in the right hemisphere and asked to name what was seen, a patient would not be able to say it in words. But, when asked to *point* out what had been seen, the patient could easily point with the left hand —controlled by the minor hemisphere—to a nearby banana, or even to the written word "banana" when presented with a list of words from which to choose. Verbal requests to find an item could be performed by the left hand easily enough, so some linguistic comprehension is present even though the minor hemisphere is unable to initiate any speech.

More testing of the minor hemisphere's linguistic capabilities has produced some remarkable results. It could not follow a simple command to smile or nod; it could not comprehend pluralization, passives, or future tense; it could not respond to verbs, adjectives, or nouns derived from verbs (e.g., "teller," "locker"). It could, however, deal with negative or affirmative constructions and respond appropriately to concrete nouns. Speech production, then, can only be initiated by the dominant hemisphere. Both hemispheres, though, are capable of language comprehension—the left with complete comprehension and the right with only partial comprehension.

One explanation for these results is that hemispheric dominance is a product of maturation, beginning in the first stages of language acquisition—around two years of age —and being completed sometime between the ages of five and twelve. Thus the limited but definitely established comprehension in the minor hemisphere could be based on elementary linguistic facts that had been acquired before lateralization took place in the individual—before language functions had been transferred completely to the dominant hemisphere.

Conjecturing more freely, it might be suggested that early stages of language included forms of a concrete nominal nature

before actual verbs were separated out from them as distinctly encoded forms. This does not contradict the speculations of some that naming things in the environment was the first important linguistic step on the way to man. It surely does contradict the "verb theory" referred to in chapter 2, however.

Research in brain anatomy and physiology has been going on for a long time, and only a brief selection of results has been presented here, in perhaps oversimplified form at that, because my purpose has been to focus on results that might relate to hominid evolution of linguistic capacities. The most apparent cognitive-linguistic changes in brain function as man evolved seem to be grounded in the development of complex intermodal association areas involving neocortex, in expanded frontal lobes that might have inhibitory relationships with the limbic system, and in lateralization.

VOCAL APPARATUS AND FOSSIL MAN

If the brain has been modified in the course of evolution, so, too, has the vocal tract. Again the chimpanzee represents something like our more direct prehominid and early hominid ancestors. We have shorter jaws and a wider and deeper pharynx. The tension of our vocal cords can be more finely controlled as can our tongue movements, and less apparent changes have also been affected. These developments have decided disadvantages for the primary functions of the speech organs, breathing, chewing, and swallowing. Apparently their only adaptive value has been for the overlaid function of speech, providing for acoustic stability and the articulation of a wide variety of distinctive sounds. And this may be a key to finding out when man began to speak. Philip Lieberman thinks so.[3]

3. Philip Lieberman, *On the Origins of Language* (New York: Macmillan Publishing Co., Inc., 1975).

According to Lieberman, Neanderthals were very inefficient speakers, who were able to transmit information at only about a tenth the rate of modern man because they lacked the ability to articulate three crucially important vowels. Right or wrong, Lieberman and his collaborators came to this conclusion in anything but an arbitrary way. First they constructed a model of a classic Neanderthal's vocal tract from the cast of a fossil skull. Then they used a computer program to determine what kinds of sounds could have come from such a vocal tract. It turned out that, like chimpanzees and newborn humans, Neanderthals would have been unable to produce the three vowels, [a], [i], and [u]. If the model accurately depicted Neanderthal's vocal tract and if this sample represented the Neanderthal population as a whole, then there should be no problem in accepting the conclusion that Neanderthal lacked these three vowels. Many have argued, however, that none of these vowels are necessary for language, that all one needs is a few consonants and a single vowel to carry the syllables.

Lieberman's view to the contrary is that these vowels are the crucial ones. This view stems from his conviction that speech perception is minimally based on the syllable and that the listener must be able to infer the size of a speaker's vocal tract in order to correctly interpret vowels and their adjacent consonants. Consonants are demonstrably perceivable primarily through transitions to adjacent vowels. Only three vowels, [a], [i], and [u] allow for good inferences about vocal tract size because they are the only stable vowel sounds produced by independent manipulations of the two vocal cavities, pharyngeal and oral. In essence, then, given this theory of speech perception, sometimes called the motor theory of speech perception, it is the presence or absence of two independent vocal cavities of sufficient size that allows one to deduce the linguistic capabilities of fossil man. Since the pharynx is what got wider and deeper in man, this seems to be the deciding factor.

SUMMARY

Chimpanzee communication both in the wild and in captivity is not of a wholly different order from that of man, particularly when viewed functionally. The systemic design feature differences between them and us may also be more a matter of degree than of kind. In some respects the chimpanzee's communicative abilities and behaviors parallel those of a two-year-old human child, but they are expressed in gesture rather than in acquired sounds. We have also seen that the human brain, though elaborated in several ways, is founded on earlier structural plans. It seems to have developed a separate referential vocal speech system that still interacts with an expressive vocalization system inherited from prelinguistic times. Inhibitory mechanisms in the brain, new cortical tissue and connections, and cerebral dominance must have developed quite slowly and in conjunction with one another over a period of many thousands or possibly millions of years. A couple of mutations just wouldn't do it. The application of one theory of speech perception to reconstructed vocal tracts constitutes a new lead in the search for language origins. It also promises more experimental research on the theory and the development of new techniques for approximating soft parts which have disappeared from skulls. Perhaps none of these roads to glottogenesis has arrived yet, but they still seem to be pointing the way.

For Further Reading

Gazzaniga, Michael S. *The Bisected Brain.* New York: Appleton-Century-Crofts, 1970. This is a book-length summary of split-brain research, engagingly written.

Jay, Phyllis C., ed. *Primates.* New York: Holt, Rinehart and Winston, 1968. This anthology contains a selection of nineteen papers on primate behavior including some fascinating observations on chimpanzee communication.

Schrier, A. M. and Stollnitz F., eds. *Behavior of Nonhuman Primates,* vol. 4. New York: Academic Press, 1971. This volume has detailed reports on Washoe, Sarah, and Viki.

Bibliography

D'Aquili, Eugene 1972. *The Biopsychological Determinants of Culture.* Addison-Wesley Modular Publications 13.

Gardner, R. A. and Gardner, B. T. 1969. "Teaching Sign Language to a Chimpanzee." *Science* 165:664-72.

Gazzaniga, Michael S. 1967. "The Split Brain in Man." *Scientific American* 217:24-29.

Geschwind, Norman. 1970. "The Organization of Language and the Brain." *Science* 170: 940-44.

Hill, Jane H. 1972. "On the Evolutionary Foundations of Language." *American Anthropologist* 74:308-17.

Jerison, H. J. 1970. "Brain Evolution: New Light on Old Principles." *Science* 170:1224-5.

Luria, A. R. 1966. *Higher Cortical Functions in Man.* New York: Basic Books, Inc.

Penfield, Wilder and Roberts, Lamar 1959. *Speech and Brain-Mechanisms.* Princeton: Princeton University Press.

Premack, David 1972. "Language in Chimpanzees?" *Science* 172:808-22.

6 | Evolution

In child language, stop phonemes generally emerge before fricatives, and these in turn emerge before affricates. Among the languages of the world, languages that have affricate phonemes also have fricatives, and languages that have fricatives also have stops. These statements represent two quite different ways of arriving at a sequential order, but the order in both ends up being the same, stop-fricative-affricate. The first statement is a developmental one entailing a chronological sequence of stages; the second is a basically typological one entailing synchronic groupings and only *implying* a sequence of stages.

If similar developmental and typological stages relating to language can be found, then it is only a short step to speculating that the same ordering of elements might apply to evolutionary stages in the emergence of language, and we have already seen that exactly this reasoning underlies many of the theories proposed in the past. In this chapter I want to consider some of the developmental evidence for evolutionary stages provided by studies in language acquisition and some of the typological evidence from studies in language universals. When these lines of evidence independently concur in a particular ordering of stages it may not always be convincing, but it is suggestive.

LANGUAGE ACQUISITION

Eric Lenneberg has pointed out an interesting and quite possibly cross-culturally valid sequence of milestones in motor and vocal development of the child which makes a good springboard for describing stages in language acquisition.[1] Chronological ages are only averaged approximations and should not be taken literally.

1. By the end of twelve weeks the child can support his head with open hands and weight on elbows while lying down. He cries less and responds to his parents by smiling and by *cooing* vowellike sounds varying in pitch for up to twenty seconds at a time.

2. By sixteen weeks the child can hold his head up while lying down and plays with rattles or other toys by looking at or touching them. He is more obviously responding to human sounds, and occasionally chuckles.

3. By twenty weeks the child can sit up with props and has begun to make a few consonantlike sounds interspersed with cooing.

4. By six months the child uses hand support while sitting and grasps things without

1. Eric Lenneberg, *Biological Foundations of Language* (New York: John C. Wiley and Sons, 1967), pp. 128-29.

use of his thumb. Cooing has changed into *babbling*, with a radical increase in consonantlike sounds. There are few restrictions on the sounds that the child makes, but some of the more frequent ones are sounds like *ma, da, mu,* or *di.*

5. By eight months the child can pick up a pellet between thumb and forefingers and can stand if holding on to something. He repeats syllables more frequently and begins to have some recognizable intonation contours. His vocalizations may signal specific emotional states or emphasis.

6. By twelve months the child can walk when held by the hand or propel himself on hands and feet with knees in the air. He replicates the same syllable sequences more frequently when vocalizing and words begin at this time to emerge, words like "bye-bye" or "mama." By this time he shows understanding of several words and responds to simple questions or commands, like "where is your nose?" His comprehension, in fact, will precede his production throughout his life. He progressively acquires a vocabulary of word-sentences or holophrastic utterances which are highly fluid in meaning and totally dependent on the immediate perceptual context. The earliest holophrases such as "hi," "bye-bye," or "hmm" appear to be integral parts of actions performed gesturally. Soon the names of persons are added, such as "Mama" or "Dudi" which are at first used only when the person is not visible but can be heard. After this, vocative or attention calling functions attend words, as when the child says "Mama" to catch his mother's attention. Somewhat later holophrastic utterances seem to refer to desired objects, as in "mik" indicating a request for milk.

7. By eighteen months the child has a fully developed grasp and slightly awkward gait. He crawls down stairs backwards. By now he has a definite repertoire of sentence-words, usually less than fifty but more than three. Some babbling is interspersed with words in an apparent imitation of speech. Following the appearance of names for things as objects of demands, such names are used in reference to objects of direct actions as in "dolly" when he sees his mother pick up a doll. After this, the child will indicate the instrument of a direct action as well, like when he says "poon" while watching someone eat with a spoon. Words may be used, but subtle gestural and postural indicators convey much information that later becomes coded into words. Comprehension of language is progressing rapidly all during this time.

8. By twenty-four months the child can run, but still may fall when turning suddenly. He can walk up or down stairs, but only one foot forward at a time. Vocabulary has grown to more than fifty words, sometimes considerably more. The child begins to join previously independent vocabulary items into two and sometimes three-word phrases of his own creation. Word order signals different grammatical relations. At this time there is an obviously increased interest in language and in communication.

9. By thirty months the child can jump up with both feet, tiptoe a bit, and stand on one foot for a couple of seconds. Babbling has stopped and most utterances have communicative intent. The child gets frustrated when not understood by adults. Vocabulary has increased by leaps and bounds, adding several new words every day. Utterances run up to about five words long on occasion. Content words without inflections make up most sentences, and function words are usually omitted.

10. By three years the child can tiptoe well, run smoothly, and climb stairs alternating feet. His vocabulary has reached around 1000 items or more, and the majority of utterances can be understood even by strangers. There are some grammatical mistakes, but function words and inflections are mostly present.

11. By four years of age the child can hop on one foot or catch a ball in his arms. Language is reasonably well established by this time. There is no trouble communicating needs or desires, but a number of syntactic and sociolinguistic rules have yet to be acquired.

Phonology

Once a child has established a small repertoire of words, by around twelve months of age, it is possible to begin studying successive stages of phonological development in terms of phonemic systems. In what we could call phonemic Stage 1, the child's system should consist of a labial, dental, and oral stop, and a single low back vowel (e.g., /p, t, m, a/). Stage 2 begins with a splitting of the single vowel into two, one high and one low (e.g., /a, i/). A labial and dental fricative may have entered the system by now, and a voicing contrast as well. Stage 3 sees the vowel system splitting into three phonemes, either /i, u, a/ or /i, e, a/. The differentiations that continue from here greatly multiply the complexity of any description, so here are a few generalizations that seem to apply cross-culturally. Stops emerge before corresponding fricatives and these emerge before corresponding affricates (e.g., /t/ before /s/ before /č/); nasals precede affricates (e.g., /n/ before /č/); liquids follow stops and nasals (e.g., /t/ before /n/ before /l/); and oral vowels precede nasalized vowels (e.g., /a/ precedes /a/).

One hypothesis about phonological development that fits quite well with these sequences was advanced by Roman Jakobson, a Prague School linguist, who proposed that children don't acquire phonemes. Instead they acquire features such as voicing, nasality, or affrication, one at a time by which they make successive differentiations among phonemic categories that have been previously undifferentiated. The very first feature contrast made, according to Jakobson, is that between vowels and consonants. Although in this limited phonemic system any consonant might occur phonetically, it will not be distinguished from any other and will be simply an allophone of the phoneme that we could label /p/. Similarly any vowel actually pronounced will be an allophone of /a/ at this point. The reason for selecting /p/ and /a/ to represent these phonemes is that they are the prototypic manifestations of maximum consonantality and vocality respectively. Successive feature distinctions applied to these phoneme categories will then differentiate them into successively finer subdivisions until phonemes with the normal adult range of allophony are arrived at. This hypothesis was proposed in conjunction with another two: first that the earliest contrasts made by children would coincide with the commonest contrasts made in languages of the world, and second that the order of feature acquisition by children would be the opposite order to that of feature loss as observed in patients beginning to suffer some forms of aphasia. In a general way these things go together in exactly the way Jakobson predicted.

Grammar

At around the age of two years a child begins forming rudimentary sentences by putting two words together. Just as in the earlier holophrastic stage, these simple utterances are by themselves very ambiguous, so the child still has to rely heavily on context, gesture, and intonation to convey his meaning. Nevertheless, word order in these two word utterances is not random; it expresses grammatical relationships between the two words. That is why people often refer to this two word stage as the beginning of grammar and hence of true language.

Roger Brown, a psychologist who has studied children for many years, has defined five stages in a child's grammatical development from two word sentences to sentences averaging four words, corresponding very roughly to the period between ages two and three years. These stages show children first using word order to express meanings, then starting to add inflections and a couple of function words, then some basic transformations, then embedding one sentence within another, and finally coordinating simple sentences. Chronological age is an unreliable indicator of when and how fast any given child will pass through a particular stage, but Brown has found that the average number of morphemes per utterance is a reasonably good predictor of stage attained. Stages 1 through 5 go from 1.75 through 4 morphemes per average utterance.

Stage 1 reflects a child's concern with marking semantic *Relations or Roles* within the simple sentence, and this is accomplished by word order. Predication—specifying attributes of things—which in the holophrastic stage was only implied, becomes overt. The meanings that children all around the world seem to express with two words in stage 1 comprise a small and basic set, as illustrated here with examples.

Identification	"see doggie"
Repetition	"more milk"
Nonexistence	"allgone candy"
Negation	"not wolf"
Location	"book there"
Possession	"my candy"
Attribution	"little doggie"
Question	"where ball?"
Agent-Action	"Mommy push"
Agent-Object	"Mommy (cuts a) pumpkin"
Action-Location	"sit chair"
Action-Direct Object	"cut pumpkin"
Action-Indirect Object	"give Papa"
Action-Instrument	"cut knife"

Stage 2 commences when the child begins to mark *Modulations of Meaning* within the simple sentence. These modulations are the kinds of changes in the meaning of content words that are made by inflectional affixes, such function words as prepositions and determiners, or by internal changes in roots: they change word meanings in terms of possession, location, direct object, number, aspect, tense, and so on. In general affixes, especially suffixes, appear in child speech before function words. A bilingual child learning one language that expresses location with suffixes while simultaneously learning another expressing location with prepositions, will have acquired the suffixes of the first well before catching on to the prepositions in the second.

When a particular affix or function word first appears in child speech it is not used consistently. In fact the child is well into Stage 5 before the major inflections and functors are present consistently and correctly. Roger Brown found that a criterion of consistency was attained by three American children in a particular order for fourteen of these "grammatical morphemes." By the end of Stage 2 the children had mastered the present progressive "-*ing*" and the prepositions "in" and "on." In Stage 3 the plural, past irregular, possessive, uncontractible copula, and articles were mastered. The past regular and third person regular endings on verbs became fixed in Stage 4, and Stage 5 saw mastery of the irregular third person, uncontractible auxiliary, contractible copula, and the contractible auxiliary.

Stage 3 is signalled when the child begins to grammatically mark all the major *Modalities* of the simple sentence. In English these modalities distinguish the basic sentence types referred to as yes-no questions ("Did Mommy come back?"), wh-questions ("Who cut the rope?"), negatives ("I don't want it"), and imperatives ("Take me with you!") from the simple declarative sentence. Typically they can be generated from declarative sentences by means of such transformation rules as word reordering, deletion, copying, and substitution. For example, "Who cut the rope" can be seen as derived from the declarative "Daddy cut the rope" by simply a substitution of the question word "who" for the constituent needing specification, in this case "Daddy." Previous to Stage 3 the child had to rely on intonation contours, gestures, and context to get the modalities of meaning across.

Stage 4 is when the child starts *Embedding* one sentence within another. What happens here is that a whole simple sentence when embedded in another becomes simply a grammatical constituent or semantic role of the other. For example, in the sentence "I hope I don't hurt it" the *I don't hurt it* part functions only as the semantic role "object" of the "I hope." Embedding can either be simple embedding where the embedded sentence is stuck on the end of the main one as in "I hope I don't hurt it," or it can be self-embedding where the embedded sentence is stuck in the middle of the main one as in "the man who came to dinner stayed a week." Simple embedding is easier for people than self-embedding.

Stage 5 sees children *Coordinating* two or more simple sentences with "and," "but," "because," and so on, all approximating in meaning the relations of propositional logic. Simple coordination of full sentences ("I found it here and I put it there") is naturally easier than coordination with appropriate deletion of constituents ("I found it here and put it there"), which is easier in turn than when more transformations are involved (e.g., He found it because he wanted to"). Also some relations of coordination such as "and" are used earlier than others such as "but."

Stages 1 through 5 show, then, a developmental order in linguistic means by which a semantic notion is expressed. In the period prior to Brown's Stage 1, the child first had to rely on context, gestures, and nonlinguistic vocalizations alone to communicate. The holophrastic stage decreased his reliance on these things by a small amount as a greater share of the communicative burden was placed on individual words and intonation. And then other linguistic means took over some of the earlier semantic functions: word order, morpheme addition to words and sentences, morpheme rearrangements, sentence embedding, and sentence coordination in that order.

Some Universals of Acquisition

Language acquisition data, though the amount and quality varies, is available on at least fifty different languages of the world. From this data a few acquisition sequences have been extracted and generalized by psychologist Dan Slobin. They include the following:

1. Suffixes precede prefixes, which precede infixes.

2. Expressions of location and direction precede expressions of time.

3. Negative expressions functioning to indicate nonexistence precede those indicating rejection which precede those indicating denial.

4. Present tense is expressed in child utterances before other time perspectives (e.g., past and future tenses).

5. Counterfactuals, conditionals, and hypotheticals are expressed relatively late in development.

6. In languages having case and gender agreement between adjective and noun, case agreement precedes gender agreement.

If you choose to treat any of these developmental sequences as clues to evolutionary ones, I won't try to stop you. Surely some of them are very suggestive.

LANGUAGE UNIVERSALS

Some features or characteristics are common to all known languages, and indeed some among these are definitional characteristics. All languages have nouns (words or larger constructions that are nominal) and verbs as well as corresponding modifiers of these two classes, adjectives and adverbs. All languages have ways of turning verbs into nouns and creating adjectives from other constituent types. All languages can turn declarative sentences into questions, commands, and negatives. Furthermore all languages have color terms, kinship terms, pronouns, place-names, terms for the body parts, terms for plants and animals, verbs of motion, and many other lexical classes. All languages have two or more vowels and eight or more consonants, and all languages have syntactic rules for hierarchically grouping linear strings of morphemes. These all could be called *unrestricted universals.*

There is another kind of language universals, *implicational universals,* which involves a relationship between two characteristics, neither of which has to be present in all languages. A typical formulation of this kind of universal assertion would be, "if a language has X characteristic, then it will also have Y, but not necessarily vice versa." For example, if a language has nasalized vowels (as Portuguese does), then it also will be found to have oral or nonnasalized vowels (as Portuguese does), and this will hold true for any language in the world. What makes it interesting is that there are many languages that have only oral vowels and no nasalized ones. Oral vowels are not simply more widespread than nasalized ones; the latter don't occur in languages without the former. In other words there is something more "basic" or "natural" about oral vowels. Similar implicational universals have been showing up in all realms of linguistic expression, from phonology to sociolinguistic routines.

Phonology

Consider this short list of some implica-

tional universals in phonology. You may want to check back with the phonetic chart in chapter 1.

1. Languages with front rounded vowels also have front unrounded and back rounded vowels.
2. Languages with fricatives also have stops.
3. Languages with affricates also have fricatives.
4. Languages with voiced obstruents also have voiceless ones.
5. Languages with voiceless continuants also have voiced ones.
6. Languages with labialized consonants also have plain ones.
7. Languages with implosive segments also have nonimplosive ones.
8. Languages with glottalized consonants also have nonglottalized ones.
9. Languages with back consonants also have front ones.

Notice the similarity here to developmental stages in child language. What relationship exists between acquisition order and implicational universals? Are the two kinds of ordering, when similar, reflections of a single underlying cause? If so, we might want to say that the underlying cause is some kind of universal human perceptual organization, genetically based and involving strategies for processing sounds which determine the direction of category differentiation. This hypothesis would appear to explain implicational universals in almost directly evolutionary terms in that sound change could be seen as the instigator of differentiation by features and language acquisition could place limits on how far it might go. This sounds something like Swadesh's self-correcting mechanism of phonetic symbolism, doesn't it?

Grammar

By 1963 Joseph Greenberg was ready to summarize a series of conclusions about language that he had reached from a sample of thirty languages and a lot of experience with others. He stated these conclusions as universals of grammar. His may have been the single most influential paper from a conference that sparked a vast amount of research in crosscultural linguistic universals. For the first half of this century most linguistic efforts were directed toward discovering all of the various ways in which languages differ from one another, and the tremendous differences discovered had led to an extremely relativistic viewpoint—one that essentially said that any concept could be coded in almost any way in some language or another. Few people outside of the Prague School in Czechoslovakia thought of finding where the limits to linguistic variability were. But there are limits as we are discovering.

Greenberg suggested an initial typology of languages based on the dominant order of S(ubject), O(bject), and V(erb) in declarative sentences. Although there are six possible orders of these three elements in a sentence—SVO, SOV, VSO, VOS, OSV, and OVS—he found that only the first three actually occurred in languages as the dominant order, with perhaps some insignificant exceptions. Because in the last three of these logically possible orders the subject follows the object, he proposed as his first universal that the subject almost always precedes the object in declarative sentences of all languages.

There are some very striking differences between VSO languages such as Berber, Maori, Welch, Zapotec, Masai, and Hebrew and VOS languages like Burmese, Japanese, Turkish, Hindi, Basque, Chibcha, and Quechua. With a couple of exceptions, they split right down the middle on several important structural features.

VSO LANGUAGES	SOV LANGUAGES
1. prepositions	postpositions
2. noun-adjective order	adjective-noun order
3. question particle initial	question particle final
4. auxiliary-main verb order	main verb-auxiliary order
5. prefixes and suffixes	suffixes only
6. common noun-proper noun	proper noun-common noun

English, like Finnish, Swahili, Thai, Yoruba, and Italian, is an SVO dominant language. With respect to the features that separate VSO from SOV, most of the SVO languages are like VSO languages, but they are less consistent as a group. The correlations uncovered by this typology led to several more proposed universals, for example:

1. Languages with dominant VSO order are always prepositional.

2. If a language has dominant SOV order and the genitive follows the governing noun, then the adjective also follows the noun.

3. If a language is exclusively suffixing, it has postpositions; if it is exclusively prefixing, it has prepositions.

In addition, Greenberg proposed some implicational universals concerning inflectional categories, like the following:

4. Person-number categories imply tense-mode categories on the verb.

5. Gender categories imply tense-mode categories on the verb.

6. Trial number implies dual number which implies plural on the noun.

7. Gender implies number on the noun.

8. Gender distinctions in the plural of the pronoun implies gender distinctions in the singular.

In all, forty-five grammatical universals were proposed in the same paper. Since that time, detailed investigations into language universals have turned up many more, but the above examples are already enough to demonstrate some parallels with the language acquisition data.

71

Lexical Universals

Implicational universals have also been uncovered in the area of vocabulary, two domains, color and botanical names, having already yielded particularly fascinating results. Research is continuing in these domains, but the most striking generalizations relating to the evolution of language have already been obtained.

Imagine being told by a friend returning from a visit to the Toda tribe in South India that these people have only three color terms. Could you tell your friend what colors they have? Brent Berlin and Paul Kay could. These anthropologists have proposed, on the basis of carefully considered ethnographic comparisons, that color terminologies of the world can be grouped on a partially ordered implicational scale such that if a society has a word for some particular color, other specifiable color terms are implied. This means that they have been able to propose a series of seven evolutionary stages through which languages necessarily pass in acquiring basic terms for the eleven focal colors that we know as black, white, red, green, yellow, blue, brown, purple, pink, orange, and gray.

To get at the basic color vocabulary in a language we have to strip away the myriad superficial ways of talking about color that might also be encoded linguistically. Such terms as blond, crimson, blue-green, greenish, or lemon-colored must be eliminated at the outset using four criteria for identifying a basic color term: (1) its meaning should not be predictable from the meaning of its parts; (2) it cannot be a kind of any other color, in the way that crimson is a kind of red, but not vice versa; (3) it cannot apply only to a narrow class of objects; and (4) it should appear among the first terms given by an informant asked to name the color terms. Once this has been done, the basic color vocabulary can be placed into one of the seven stages shown here. What makes this possible is that people all over the world pick the same colors as most representative foci for their basic color terms.

Stage 1 black, white
Stage 2 black, white, red
Stage 3a black, white, red, green
Stage 3b black, white, red, yellow
Stage 4 black, white, red, yellow, green
Stage 5 black, white, red, yellow, green, blue
Stage 6 black, white, red, yellow, green, blue, brown
Stage 7 black, white, red, yellow, green, blue, brown, purple, pink, orange, gray

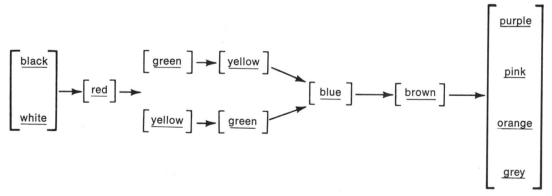

Figure 6.1 BASIC COLOR TERMS

You will have noticed that Stage 3 is divided into two alternative possibilities. Some languages pass through Stage 3a and others through Stage 3b. No language passes through both. The order in which a language acquires purple, pink, orange, and gray is similarly unspecifiable. They often seem to come into a language pretty much at the same time. The sequence in which languages acquire basic color terms can also be diagrammed as in figure 6.1.

Recent work by Berlin among the Aguaruna of Peru has led to a slight alteration in this postulated evolutionary sequence, and to another significant insight—that although contact between societies having quite different stages of color vocabulary can modify the terminology of the earlier stage, "where basic color vocabulary can be shown to be changing due to culture contact, basic color terms will be acquired in the identical order by which they are added diachronically in the evolutionary development of languages generally."[2] It is interesting to note that other researchers have demonstrated a correlation between the color evolutionary sequence and the length of terms as well as their frequency of use.

Berlin has also suggested an evolutionary sequence in the emergence of categories of botanical nomenclature in languages. To do this he investigated botanical terminologies in several cultures and found that six universal categories of plant names would have to be distinguished in order to describe the taxonomic structure in botanical vocabularies for any language: (1) generic, (2) specific, (3) major life form, (4) varietal, (5) intermediate, and (6) unique beginner. Here are examples of five of these categories in our own folk nomenclature; named intermediate categories tend to be unstable, arising primarily through culture contact and being lost relatively rapidly, so it is difficult to find examples.

Unique Beginner	"plant"
Major Life Form	"tree," "grass," "vine"
Intermediate	[no example]
Generic	"oak," "pipevine," "pine"
Specific	"white oak," "pinon pine"
Varietal	"weeping piñon pine"

These categories appear in the life histories of languages with named representatives in a relatively fixed sequence, which can be shown in figure 6.2.

The ordering here is only partial as you can see. The diagram shows, for example, no prediction for chronological precedence be-

2. Brent Berlin and Elois Ann Berlin, "Aguaruna Color Categories," *American Ethnologist* 2 (1975):83.

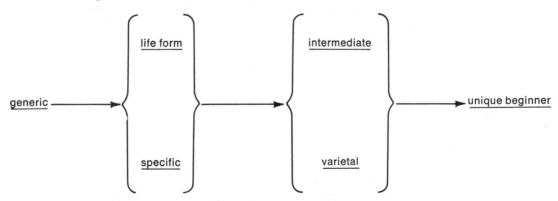

Figure 6.2 ETHNOBOTANICAL CATEGORY SEQUENCE

tween Life Form and Specific categories; but at least one labelled member of each must have appeared in the language before Intermediate or Varietal terms appear if the sequence is correct. Each of these categories, excepting the Unique Beginner, is essentially an open class that can gain or lose terms throughout a language's history. Notice the implications of this postulated sequence. It means that languages in later stages (i.e., further along in the sequence) have more concrete *and* more abstract labelled categories, at least in the domain of botanical nomenclature.

Further work on terminological systems, including anatomical terms, zoological terms, and pronominal terms has already begun. If, as Berlin appears to have shown, there are aspects of the human lexicon that evolve in a regularly patterned manner, it should not be too long before causal explanations are forthcoming.

Sociolinguistic Universals

Very little has been done explicitly in the area of sociolinguistic universals.[3] Some things, nevertheless, appear as obvious candidates for speculations about universality, as hypotheses to be tested. One might propose, for example, that:

1. All societies have sex-role marked distinctions in speech, linguistic means for expressing respect, spoken greetings, apologies, thanks, casual and formal speech varieties, sacred expressions and slang, conventionalized gestural expressions, and language specific subphonemic expressive conventions.

2. If a language lexically encodes status distinctions, then it will also lexically encode sex-role distinctions.

3. If a society has status ranking, then higher ranked persons will have norms of role behavior calling for formal speech va-

rieties in a greater number of social contexts.

These examples illustrate only a small segment of apparently limitless possibilities for sociolinguistic universals. Organizing this area could be very important for our understanding of the origins of language because sociolinguistic inquiry necessitates a functional perspective, and because language as part of culture evolved in human society, which means that social needs have helped to determine linguistic form and variation.

Paul Kay has advanced two hypotheses on the evolution of language that neatly tie together the strands of evolutionary diversification, variation, and social needs in evolving societies. In essence his argument runs something like the following.

In our modern society we find two fundamentally different varieties of spoken communication, autonomous and nonautonomous. *Nonautonomous speech* is heavily supported by gestures and context, more fluent, syntactically less complex, less edited, and very much less explicitly informative in terms of the linguistic form. Nonautonomous speech depends greatly on the hearer to fill in from background knowledge those aspects of the message not made explicit by the speaker. In short, nonautonomous speech is adapted to situations involving persons with similar background knowledge, frequent interaction, and intimate relationships.

Autonomous speech, on the other hand, is more syntactically complex, more linguistically explicit, less dependent on paralinguistic and kinesic signals, and less dependent on background information pos-

---

3. Two anthropologists, Penny Brown and Stephen Levinson, are currently engaged in some of the most promising work in this area, particularly with respect to politeness phenomena. The more general development of sociolinguistics is most closely associated with the names Erving Goffman, John Gumperz, Susan Ervin-Tripp, and Dell Hymes.

sessed by the hearer. The greater the psychological difference between communicating individuals, the greater the need for autonomous speech.

The evolution of human societies has certainly been in the direction of increasing complexity, of increasing numbers of different kinds of social situations, of increasing numbers of people living in the same communities, of social differentiation. This results in more and more situations calling for autonomous speech because increasingly smaller percentages of people having to communicate will share the common experiences and understandings necessary for nonautonomous speech to be successful.

Kay's first hypothesis, then, is that linguistic evolution has been in the direction of autonomous systems of symbols. The second is that a major evolutionary mechanism shaping this direction has been adaptation of our communicative systems to increasingly complex and diversified speech communities.

SUMMARY

The data on linguistic universals and language acquisition can be arranged in developmental sequences. Sequences derived from both of these areas agree in some striking respects. More generally they indicate development by differentiation from simple systems to complex systems. Language acquisition proceeds from total dependence on context for message interpretation to lessening degrees of such dependence as linguistic symbols are acquired to make messages more explicit and independent of shared experience. The linguistic development of the child gives all the appearance of an individual adapting to situations calling for autonomous speech by learning a linguistic system which can make maximally explicit and independent of context the messages he wants to convey. Fortunately

he has considerable genetic help in this adaptation, one suspects.

For Further Reading

Berlin, Brent and Kay, Paul *Basic Color Terms*. Berkeley: University of California Press, 1969. This short book contains the methodology and evidence for the evolution of color terminologies.

Brown, Roger *A First Language*. Cambridge: Harvard University Press, 1973. Anyone wanting to know most of the recent issues and results in language acquisition studies should read this clearly written book.

Greenberg, Joseph, ed. *Universals of Language*. 2d ed. Cambridge: MIT Press, 1966. This is still the best single book on language universals. It contains eleven articles by leaders in several fields, and some of them make difficult reading.

———. *Language Universals*. The Hague: Mouton & Co., 1966. This booklet sees universals from the standpoint of a generalized theory of linguistic markedness, illustrating the application of markedness to phonology, grammar, and lexicon.

Ferguson, Charles and Slobin, Dan, eds. *Studies in Child Language Development*. New York: Holt, Rinehart and Winston, 1973. This excellent reader contains important reprints and a long chapter by Slobin on universals in language acquisition.

Bibliography

Bach, Emmon and Harms, Robert T., eds. 1968. *Universals in Linguistic Theory*. New York: Holt, Rinehart and Winston.

Berlin, Brent 1972. "Speculations on the Growth of Ethnobotanical Nomenclature." *Language in Society* 1:51-86.

Berlin, Brent and Berlin, Elois Ann 1975. "Aguaruna Color Categories." *American Ethnologist* 2:61-88.

Goffman, Erving 1971. *Relations in Public.* New York: Basic Books, Inc.

Hill, Jane H. and Hill, Kenneth C. 1970. "A Note on Uto-Aztecan Color Terminologies." *Anthropological Linguistics* 12:231-38.

Huxley, Renira and Ingram, Elisabeth, eds. 1971. *Language Acquisition: Models and Methods.* New York: Academic Press.

Slobin, Dan I. 1972. "They Learn the Same Way All Around the World." *Psychology Today,* May, pp. 71-74.

———. 1972. *Leopold's Bibliography of Child Language.* Bloomington: Indiana University Press.

Werner, Heinz and Kaplan, Bernard 1967. *Symbol Formation.* New York: John C. Wiley & Sons, Inc.

7 | Conclusions

In the preceding chapters we have seen many pathways that may lead to a deeper understanding of what language is and how it evolved. Currently most of the paths are being explored in one way or another, and many researchers in divergent fields, often without realizing it, are digging up information of relevance; but we have to know where to look. I can think of thirteen different avenues that have been probed for insights into glottogenesis. Most of them have already been mentioned or discussed in preceding chapters—a couple, though, have not. Enumerating them here will give me the opportunity to rationalize, justify, or expand on things I didn't say earlier. They follow in no particularly revealing order.

Language Acquisition

Looking to developmental sequences for an understanding of evolutionary ones has been scoffed at by many reputable persons. They repeatedly point out that ontogeny does not in fact recapitulate phylogeny as was once believed. True enough, in biology at least; the individual does not pass through the adult stages of evolutionary ancestors in the course of his ontogenetic development, but he often *does* pass through ancestral *developmental* stages. Evolution builds piece by piece on structural plans that are already there, and in the individual's ontogenetic development many ancestral plans of structure and process are genetically retained. Thus it is possible for ontogenetic transformations to reveal some of the earlier structural plans on which evolution built. But then we are not really talking directly about biology anyhow when we look at language development to learn about language evolution.

This does not mean that we should be incautious about interpreting evidence from language acquisition studies. There is no guarantee that they tell us anything about language evolution. The developing child is not inventing language but simply learning a particular language that is already there. With proper caution, however, it seems perfectly legitimate to me to at least make use of this obvious and most intriguing area of research for clues of *possible* evolutionary sequences.

In any case, language ontogeny appears to take place through successive differentiations that could be thought of as based on the acquisition of feature contrasts, it progresses from a very nonautonomous communicative system to an autonomous one, it parallels general cognitive development in many ways, it passes through an "isolating" two-word stage with no inflections directly after a holophrastic stage of global and fluid meanings, it procedes from almost exclusively emotive and expressive to very referential in function—in appropriate contexts, of course—and it is preceded by periods when gesture and intonation constitute almost all of the communicative system.

Pidgins and Creoles

This is a subject not previously mentioned. In brief, a pidgin is a contact vernacular created in a situation where communication must take place between persons who don't speak each other's languages. It is used in limited social contexts only, such as in trading, and it is not the native language of anyone who speaks it. Pidgins all seem to share several characteristics, including a small vocabulary, few morphophonemic rules and little allophony, few if any inflections like number or gender, and a propensity to apply negation and other such qualifiers only to whole sentences or predicates. They omit many redundant features and appear to represent structural simplifications created in the interest of communication in limited social settings.

A creole also minimizes syntactic redundancy, but it has a full vocabulary and is the native language of most of its speakers. Some authorities claim that creoles invariably have descended from pidgins, but there is disagreement on this point.

Two things make the study of pidgins and creoles particularly interesting from the perspective of glottogenesis. The first is that only a few years ago the subject began to come under intensive scholarly scrutiny, and now it is a rapidly expanding field; before that it was thought worthy of linguistic attention by only very few. The second is that pidgins can be viewed as part languages created just about from scratch, or as drastically stripped down languages, and creoles can be seen as initially relatively impoverished systems that have come to be expanded and made syntactically complex enough to meet the communicative needs of native speakers. Viewing the processes involved in both pidginization and creolization should give some hints about possibly partially analogous language genesis and evolution. One thing is sure; there are at least some interesting parallels between language acquisition and the processes involved in pidginization and creolization.

Language Universals

Language universals were distinguished earlier into two kinds, unrestricted and implicational. The latter lend themselves to interpretations of sequence in terms of the differentiation of categories, whether these be phonological, grammatical, lexical, or sociolinguistic, and some of the sequences have been noted to look much like ontogenetic sequences. The former include definitional characteristics, and, of course, such characteristics specify the nature of the first stage after glottogenesis.

Nondefinitional characteristics of all languages are more difficult to evaluate. Take allophony, for example. All phonological systems have allophonic variation of phonemes, some random and some phonetically conditioned. But what inferences about linguistic evolution can we make from that fact? Presumably, very little. Or what about metaphor? Our ability to find new uses for old forms (as when we extended the meaning of "neck" from our anatomy to the analogous area on a bottle and later to the actions of young lovers) has been one of the prime movers in semantic change and is certainly a hallmark of human use of language, yet I recall no definition of language in which it explicitly figures. Ask yourself if it is possible to imagine a language in which every form has a single fixed meaning and cannot be used to refer to anything else. Another universal: every language includes some sentences that are more than ten morphemes in length. The only way I can conceive of an earlier linguistic stage in which there were, say, no sentences with more than five morphemes would be if speech processing limitations in the brain were enforcing such a limitation. All known languages have color terms and names for plants, too, but how far back in language evolution do we have to go to find a stage when there were no color terms or names for plants? If there was such a stage, would the language of that time have had at least incipient color terms?

Some nondefinitional characteristics of all languages are difficult in another way—they turn out only to be near universals when one or more languages are found lacking them. Take nasals, for example. It seems that every language in the world has nasals except for a small group of languages located in the Pacific Northwest of America.[1] Or syllable structure as another example: all languages were supposed to have syllables beginning with one or more consonants. Then in a remote corner of Australia a language was found in which all the syllables begin with vowels and end with consonants.[2] Australia provides another example of a near universal. An Australian language, Walbiri, has no system of named numerals, although the speakers can count using determiners. The question that stems naturally from these examples is, why do just a few languages lack characteristics that are otherwise universally present in languages? If such near universal features were all lacking in the same languages, then we might suspect that we had uncovered a group of languages representative in some respects of an earlier stage in linguistic evolution, but they are not, and the question remains.

It is probably universally true that men and women speak differently, and there are many languages in which male/female differences in speech are encoded directly in the phonology, lexicon, or grammar of the language. A smaller number of languages have sex-role-differentiated linguistic forms whose usage is determined not only by the sex of speaker, but also by the sex of addressee. In Yana, a language of northern California, for example, most words have both a full form and a reduced (or shorter) form. The full forms are used only by males speaking to other males.[3] Other combinations of speaker and hearer employ the reduced forms. The converse of this situation can also be seen in some other languages. Now linguistic marking of sex-role-differentiated speech has been viewed by some as a structural characteristic antecedent to the grammatical category of gender where nouns, and later verbs, come to be associated with one sex or another and are then grammatically marked for gender in and of themselves regardless of the sex of speaker or hearer. This is clearly an evolutionary hypothesis which, if true, tells us that gender categories follow rather than precede sex-differentiated speech. And just as clearly, this proposed implicational universal is sociolinguistic in nature, depending not only on referential linguistic form but also on language usage.

Focusing on function rather than form, we are led to speculate on the adaptational

1. These languages belong to three separate language families, and there may be another American Indian language, Pawnee in the Midwest, that also lacks nasals. See L. C. Thompson and M. T. Thompson, "Language Universals, Nasals, and the Northwest Coast," in *Studies in Linguistics,* ed. M. Estellie Smith (The Hague: Mouton & Co., 1972), pp. 441-56.

2. Bruce A. Sommer, "An Australian Language Without CV Syllables," *International Journal of American Linguistics* 36 (1970):57-60.

3. Edward Sapir, "Male and Female Forms of Speech in Yana," in *Selected Writings of Edward Sapir,* ed. D. Mandelbaum (Berkeley: University of California Press, 1948), pp. 206-12.

utility of language for helping man to cope with his environment. Edward Sapir pointed out eight general functions of language which have direct and interesting consequences for culture growth and societal change. First, perhaps the most evident function of language is that of communication. No need to belabor the point that with language we have a very powerful instrument for sharing our feelings and thoughts with others and a highly effective means for exchange of environmental information, which in turn makes possible increasingly complex interrelationships among individuals in a society. The communicative function of language is important, but it should also be understood that language can be an integral part of situations that are not at all obviously communicative, and that effective communication can be accomplished without overt speech. Second, language projects meaning to potential experience, allowing us to communicate about things that may never have happened and may never occur in the future. With words we can be quite precise about the size and shape of an elephant without having seen one, the speed of light without having timed it with a stopwatch, the chemical composition of Venus, the appetites of a unicorn, or the number of angels that can dance on the head of a pin. These things have meaning and become part of our cognitive experience. The design features displacement and prevarication are clearly interdependent in the context of this function of language. Third, while helping us to explore and even create reality, language is also predisposing us to observe and interpret our experience in particular ways. Time and time again psychological experimentation has shown the influence of linguistic labels on our perception of categories of experience, and it is reasonable to suppose that phonology and grammar also help to shape aspects of our customary behavior and outlook. Fourth, language functions universally as a force

for individual socialization, as an important factor in one's internalization of cultural norms for behavior. It makes us less dependent on genetic control of behavioral patterns or on learning simply by imitation. With language the individual can be taught how to behave in culturally appropriate and adaptively advantageous ways prior to actually experiencing situations calling for specific modes of behavior. Fifth, language is a reservoir for the accumulation of cultural knowledge, knowledge that helps to maintain and define the social group, and sixth, knowledge which can be transmitted from one generation to another. Traditional transmission insures a flexibility that genetic transmission does not have, allowing for extraordinarily rapid behavioral accommodation to prevailing environmental conditions. Seventh, language is also an important factor in the growth and maintenance of individuality. Everyone expresses his individuality through speech—as well as in other kinds of behavior—and thereby increases the complexity of social relationships. This complexity in turn creates situations in which explicit and unambiguous communication may be at a premium, at least up to a point. And finally, linguistic expression can also allow for the survival of individuals not so well equipped to cope with the environment through "primary action patterns." The good speaker, for example, may hold an important position in his society in spite of puniness, lameness, or other survival handicaps. Language can be a supreme instrument for adaptive adjustment to the natural and social environment by individuals lacking other behavioral skills, and so has an effect on the course of biological evolution.

What I have been getting at is that there are many sorts of language universals—universals in form, content, and function—and progress in our delineation and understanding of these universals surely contributes clues towards a better understanding of language evolution. Many of these clues reinforce those obtained in the study of language ontogeny and point to language acquisition studies as relevant for speculations on glottogenesis.

Language Typologies

Implicational universals can be derived from language typologies, but are not necessarily a part of their construction. A typology such as that illustrated in chapter 4 may only reveal cyclical rather than evolutionarily directed changes in form. Others might be more successful in representing a sequence of linguistic stages, so we should not forget the utility of typologies in any search for language origins. On the other hand, even the cyclical nature of language transformations with respect to the isolating-agglutinating-inflecting typology should not obscure its evident parallels to the language acquisition sequence.

Sapir proposed a typological classification of languages based not on word formation but on the degree to which individual languages formally and explicitly express fundamental relational concepts.[4] According to this scheme every language belongs to one of four types, and tends to retain its type characteristics over long periods of time. Sapir's suggested typology is elegant, but temptations to order the types on an evolutionary scale should be resisted until clues from other avenues converge on a plausible order. Even then we must be firmly aware of the fact that evolutionary ordering of typological categories implies the assumption that language types of today are capable of representing language stages of yesterday. It is a very large assumption.

Processes of Language Change

Some processes in language change are more natural and more common than others.

Metaphoric transfers from sound to touch, for example, are much rarer than from touch to sound. Isolating languages are more likely to become suffixing ones than prefixing ones, prefixes are more likely to merge with one another through sound change while suffixes tend to remain more stable as the root develops assimilative irregularities, and assimilation in sound change is more common than dissimilation. These are relatively short-term processes which may or may not reflect long-term overall evolutionary trends in language. They do, however, probably reflect human cognitive organization in ways that have yet to be delineated clearly and that themselves have much to do with language evolution.

One reason that short-term processes of language change have not often been interpreted in an evolutionary context is that a language's history involves opposing tendencies, both toward simplification and complexification. This follows from the communicative necessity to balance economy of expression with explicitness of expression. We can see, for example, that regular sound change often operates to erode the machinery for linguistically marking conceptual categories, and sometimes to create homonymous forms. Semantic change and analogical creations help to reestablish conceptual distinctions lost earlier and to mark them with explicit linguistic forms. This interplay among opposing tendencies in language change illustrates limits to the directionality of change and makes it difficult to trace the route of linguistic evolution from simpler to more complex.

It is possible, though, to speculate that two important processes, increasing overall redundancy and decreasing ambiguity, were operative in the earliest stages of language. Duplication of perceived environmental in-

4. Edward Sapir, *Language* (New York: Harcourt, Brace, and World, 1921), pp. 120-46.

formation in linguistic forms is the sort of redundancy I am referring to here, and the more precise and explicit a language becomes in encoding environmental information, the more redundant it becomes in this sense. Also, if we assume that language did not spring forth in fully developed form, the earliest stages had to be more ambiguous because any utterance would have to carry a greater range of possible interpretations, a selection from among fewer alternative possibilities, less information, in short.

Linguistic Reconstruction

Chapter 4 contains a discussion of some techniques for linguistic reconstruction. Most of them were seen to be limited to fairly shallow time depths, but those which weren't led to speculation about early stages of language that again parallel speculations derived from other avenues of inquiry. The comparative method applied to reconstructed protolanguages promises some interesting results; and a few attempts of this sort have been carried out already, but of course they are limited by the degree of thoroughness and accuracy with which the protolanguages themselves have been reconstructed.[5]

The comparative method leads also to interpretations of environmental features presumed to be characteristic of a protolanguage's homeland. India, for example, has been ruled out as the homeland for Proto-Indo-European speakers partly because words for monkey, fig tree, elephant, and tiger cannot be reconstructed.[6] Reconstructed forms for birch, beech, elm, yew, oak, ash, linden, hazel, juniper, apple, and alder among others suggest a homeland area north and perhaps slightly east of the Mediterranean Sea. Pollen analysis of past eras delimits overlapping areas over which each

tree genus ranged when Proto-Indo-European speakers lived. Furthermore, etymological and other evidence indicates that five trees were linked with Proto-Indo-European religion, the oak, birch, linden, yew, and beech.[7]

Linguistic reconstruction is continually being refined, and more data on various protolanguages is being produced. Although traditional methods have yet to bring us anywhere near the dawn of language there can be little doubt that the veil of time is being pushed steadily back. Less traditional methods suggest a monogenetic origin for the languages of the world and that a very early phonemic inventory included one vowel and thirteen consonants. Moreover very early stages of language relied heavily on sound symbolism to mark such conceptual categories as shape, size, proximity, and repetition if Swadesh is correct.

Design Features of Animal Communication Systems

I think that two points are very important with respect to this avenue of investigation. First, the most relevant comparisons of communication systems are between human communication and that of our closest relatives on the phylogenetic scale. Bird communication and starfish communication are of course important to understanding the nature of communication in general and perhaps can furnish hints about what to look at in ape or human commmunication, but

5. In this connection see Esther Matteson et al., *Comparative Studies in Amerindian Languages* (The Hague: Mouton & Co., 1972).

6. See Paul Thieme, "The Comparative Method for Reconstruction in Linguistics," in *Language in Culture and Society,* ed. Dell Hymes (New York: Harper & Row, Publishers, 1964), pp. 585-97.

7. Paul Friedrich, *Proto-Indo-European Trees* (Chicago: The University of Chicago Press, 1970).

these systems are not nearly so relevant for design feature comparisons with human language. Second, Hockett's design features are very useful for ordering similarities and differences between ape and human communication systems, but they are most useful when understood to represent continua rather than all-or-nothing features.

Since Hockett's delineation of design features, other features or characteristics of language have been proposed. John Lyons, for example, outlines five of what he calls the more basic semiotic functions or sign types. These are *deixis* (calling attention to contextual items not by naming them but by locating them with respect to the speaker), *vocative signals* (which attract the hearer's attention and invite his participation in situated interaction), *nomination* (the assignment of a name to something), *desiderative signals* (signals indicating an organism's desire for some object), and *instrumental signals* (which serve to accomplish specific goals).[8]

Roger Wescott identifies eighteen communicative traits that are indispensible to present-day languages, and two traits—using propositional components that have no referential meaning, and internal subordination of one proposition to another—which are present but not crucial. Presumably the latter two came late in the evolution of language.[9] He also posits an evolutionary sequence of increasing differentiation by subordination in which nouns and verbs as head-forms come to be modified by adjectives, after which function words like prepositions and conjunctions are added, and then affixes such as prefixes and suffixes, and finally zero morphemes. Reversing the postulated evolutionary order of functors and affixes, we have a sequence that mirrors the ontogenetic one.

The design features of Hockett and others may prove to be very useful in the future as they have been so far. At the minimum,

exploration of this approach has generated many new ideas about language evolution and has led to necessary clarifications of the concepts referred to as design features.

Ape Communicative and Cognitive Capabilities

This avenue logically precedes that of design features in that we still do not know enough about chimpanzee cognitive and "linguistic" potential to effectively place them on a scale of duality, openness, displacement, and so on. What we do know about chimpanzee communication, however, suggests very strongly the importance of unloading the affect from messages in language evolution, of increasing explicitness of questions and commands as well as propositional utterances, of increasing referential displacement from the specific speech situation, and of expanding capacities for analogical creation.

Chimpanzees will probably never learn to speak, but they have already demonstrated a cognitive capacity for naming, self-recognition, deixis, openness, duality of patterning, and displacement by means of gestural signals. Only the future can show how far they are capable of carrying each communicative design feature.

Speech Pathology

This avenue has been left relatively untouched in the preceding discussions, but it

8. John Lyons, "Human Language," in *Non-Verbal Communication*, ed. Robert Hinde (Cambridge: Cambridge University Press, 1972), pp. 49-85.

9. Roger W. Wescott, "The Origin of Speech," in *Language Origins,* ed. R. W. Wescott (Silver Spring, Md.: Linstok Press, 1974), pp. 103-24.

seems to have considerable potential for elucidating language acquisition processes, brain structure and functions, and perhaps language evolution. One condition, congenital anarthria, in which the patient cannot speak but can understand language demonstrates that there is a wide gulf between comprehension and production, and perhaps that comprehension is prior to and simpler than production. Another condition, mongolism, seems to arrest the linguistic development of children at "primitive" stages in normal ontogeny. Congenitally deaf children often have trouble in writing complex grammatical constructions, but it has been suggested that this is due to lack of extensive exposure to a variety of language examples.

Roman Jakobson's linking of child speech to language universals and to aphasia is of particular interest. Essentially he held that what is learned earliest is lost last and shows up in the largest number of languages of the world. As language abilities deteriorate, for whatever reason, there often seems to be a sequence of losses that runs exactly counter to the sequence of child acquisition of linguistic forms. Most evidence for Jakobson's theory comes from the area of phonology, but there is no reason not to suppose that it will be found to apply to some extent to other aspects of language. To the extent that his theory is correct and generalizable, three lines of investigation seem to be leading to similar conclusions.

Vocal Tract Anatomy and Speech Perception

These are really two distinct avenues of inquiry that were brought together by Lieberman and his coworkers. Several specimens from different time periods have now been studied and their vocal tracts reconstructed. The La-Chapelle-aux-Saints specimen of Neanderthal may represent a population

that had already diverged from the main line of human evolution, as Lieberman now suggests, for reconstructions of earlier fossil representatives including *Homo erectus* have been tentatively diagnosed as capable of essentially human articulation. *Australopithecus* has, however, been found wanting in this respect. An example of *Australopithecus africanus* seems to have had the same vocal limitations as a chimpanzee.

There is much to learn yet about speech perception, so Lieberman's conclusions are still being challenged in the technical journals. Recent studies in speech perception do tend to support the notion of feature differentiation, and they also indicate that the syllable may be the basic segment of sound that is encoded. Furthermore, they lead us directly into hypotheses about language processing in the brain.

Brain Structure and Function

This avenue is where we must go to find anatomical and physiological correlates to language. Among other things we have seen the importance of lateralization, evolutionarily recent neocortical structures, and two semi-independent speech systems in man. It has also been suggested that the development of complex suppressor and inhibitory networks was critical in language evolution,[10] and that a developmental process of neural sheathing, called myelinization, can be useful for locating evolutionarily recent areas of cerebral cortex. None of the brain data considered here conflicts with hypotheses about the autonomization of language developed from other research avenues.

10. William F. Orr and Stephen C. Cappannari, "The Emergence of Language," *American Anthropologist* 66 (1964):319-23.

Cultural Correlates Presupposing Language

Reasoning that certain complexities of culture presuppose language can lead easily into the trap of forgetting how much information can be shared without overt linguistic expression in small homogeneous communities where common experience and understandings greatly facilitate nonautonomous communication. What we need to find out is just how developed culture can get in such communities without requiring some sort of language. Careful attention to the functions of speech will be necessary in any reasonable speculations of this kind.

Extant Primitive Languages

The only hope now in this area is if the Bigfoot turns out to be real.

For Further Reading

Haugen, Einar, and Bloomfield, eds. *Language as a Human Problem.* New York: W. W. Norton Co. Inc., 1973, 1974. An excellent collection of essays written by leading scholars that approaches language from many different perspectives.

Hymes, Dell, ed. *Pidginization & Creolization of Languages.* Cambridge: Cambridge University Press, 1971. A well-conceived and edited anthology constituting the most important volume on pidgins and creoles so far.

Bibliography

DeCamp, David and Hancock, Ian F., eds. 1974. *Pidgins and Creoles: Current Trends and Prospects.* Washington, D. C.: Georgetown University Press.

Herrick, C. Judson 1956. *The Evolution of Human Nature.* Austin: University of Texas Press.

Hinde, Robert A., ed. 1972. *Non-Verbal Communication.* Cambridge: Cambridge University Press.

Huxley, Julian 1964. *Evolution: The Modern Synthesis.* New York: John C. Wiley & Sons, Inc.

Jakobson, Roman 1968. *Child Language, Aphasia, and Phonological Universals.* The Hague: Mouton.

——— 1972. "Motor Signs for 'Yes' and 'No'." *Language in Society* 1:91-96.

Lakoff, Robin 1973. "Language and Woman's Place." *Language in Society* 2:45-80.

Sapir, Edward 1921. *Language.* New York: Harcourt, Brace & World.

Glossary

Affix—Satellites to roots in grammatical constructions. An affix may be a prefix, suffix, or infix. Affixes never occur alone, and they convey less information than do roots.

Allomorph—Variant shapes of morphemes which may be phonologically conditioned or not. Allomorphs of a single morpheme are either in free variation or complementary distribution with one another, they have the same essential meaning, and they are similar in phonological shape to one another.

Article—A kind of determiner. In English "the," "an," and "a" are determiners, but there are only two of them. The "a" and "an" are phonologically conditioned allomorphs of the same morpheme.

Aspect—A grammatical category, realized as inflections or as particles, which describes the stage or type of completion of action attributable to the verb; some aspect categories are the completive, the incompletive, and the repetitive.

Auxiliary—See *Copula*.

Case—A grammatical category by which nouns in some languages are inflected to signal subject, object, agent, or other like syntactic category, and sometimes to signal distinctions of space or time. Latin, Finnish, and Russian are among the many case languages.

Cognates—Words related to each other by being descended from the same original word.

Common Noun—A noun that may refer to any or all of the members of a class of things, for example "pig," "man," or "tree."

Coordination—The relationship between two grammatical constructions that are structurally of equivalent rank. Coordination contrasts with subordination in which two grammatical constructions, whether morpheme, phrase, or sentence, are related to one another in such a manner that they are not of equivalent rank; one modifies the other, you might say.

Copula—The verb "be" in its three person-inflected forms can serve as a copula as in "He is happy" and "There it is." The former is contractible as in "He's happy" and the latter is not. The verb "be" can also be an auxiliary to a verb as in "He is running fast" or "Is he running fast?" The former is contractible and the latter is not.

Determiner—Such noun modifiers as "the," "a," "some," "this," etc. in English.

Gender—A grammatical category, gender may be masculine, feminine, or neuter, or it may be some other noun specifier as we find in many African languages. Gender need not, but often does, imply sex.

Homorganic—This means having the same place of articulation in the mouth.

Inflection—An affix or segment change in the root that specifies such things as tense, aspect, mood, etc. It does not change the stem class of a word. Inflection also refers to the process of adding inflections to words.

Lateral—A consonant articulated by obstructing the center of the mouth with the tongue and allowing the sound to emerge on either side.

Lexical Item—A word, a vocabulary item.

Liquid—A consonant that is articulated without friction but with partial obstruction of the breath stream. (r) and (l) are liquids.

Morpheme—The smallest part of an utterance that carries referential meaning.

Morphophoneme—Some morphemes have more than one phonemic shape. When these variant shapes are phonologically conditioned, they are considered to represent a single morphophoneme, provided that they are only one segment in length.

Number—A grammatical category of inflection including such things as singular, dual, trial, and plural.

Oral—Articulation of a speech sound through the mouth rather than through the nose. Also one of the three speech cavities, oral, nasal, and pharyngeal.

Paradigm—A set of items sharing some basic characteristic.

Passive—"The door was opened by John" illustrates a passive grammatical construction. This is in contrast to the active construction "John opened the door."

Position—Position in a grammatical construction is an item's privilege of occurrence.

Postposition—Similar to a preposition, but it comes after the noun. There are no examples of postpositions in English.

Prefix—A bound morpheme attached in front of roots.

Preposition—A function word preceding the noun which marks its place as well as usually carrying some semantic information, as with the prepositions "in," "on," "by," "before," etc.

Proper Noun—The name of a particular person, place, or thing, e.g., John, New York, Old Betsy.

Proto-Indo-European—A hypothetically reconstructed language which is taken to represent the common ancestor of all languages in the Indo-European language family, of which English is but one member.

Root—The nucleus of a grammatical construction, carrying a greater information load than affixes which can be attached to them. Some roots are never inflected and these are usually called particles.

Stem Class—Stem classes, like nouns, verbs, adjectives, and so on, are defined by a unique set of inflectional affixes with which they may occur. Certain affixes within this set may be shared with another stem class.

Subordination—See *coordination*.

Trial—See *number*.

Zero—The absence of an element can under some conditions be described as a zero element.

Index

active, 46
adaptation, 40
affix, 7, 68
affricate, 4, 65, 67, 70
agglutinating language, 52
Aguaruna, 73
alienable, 51
allomorph, 8
allophone, 5, 67
alternation, 17, 28
American Sign Language, 57-58
animal cry, 24
Apache, 22
aphasia, 39, 61
apology, 57-58
arbitrariness, 55
arrangement, 9
aspiration, 5, 17, 28
association areas, 60
attribution, 68
Australia, 79
Australopithecus, 28, 32-33,
    36-37, 84
autonomous speech, 74-75
Aztec, 35, 47

babbling, 23, 65-66
Babel, Tower of, 35
Basque, 71
Berber, 71
Berlin, Brent, 72-74
Berlin, Brent, and Elois Ann
    Berlin, 73
Bigfoot, 1, 85
bipedalism, 36
bird song, 21
blending, 29
blindness, 39
Bloomfield, 13
borrowing, 43, 48
botanical terms, 73-74
boundaries, 41, 43
Bow-wow theory, 21

brain stem, 59
breeding population, 41
Broca's area, 61
Brown, Penny, 74
Brown, Roger, 1, 67-68
Burmese, 71

canines, reduction, 36
Cappanari, Stephen, 84
categories, 73
cerebellum, 59
cerebrum, 58
Chibcha, 71
child language, 65-69
chimpanzees, 29, 37, 39, 55-58
Chinese, 51
chronology, 45-46
Classic language, 28
classification:
    areal, 1
    genetic, 1, 45
    typological, 1, 51-52, 81
cognates, 45
color terms, 72-73
command, 70
comparative reconstruction,
    47-49
competence, 2, 3
compound, 8
concatenation, 17
concord, 11
constituent, 69
contact function, 15
contact theory, 26
content words, 11
contextual function, 17
continuants, 70
convolutions, 60
co-occurrence, 11, 17
cooing, 65
cooperation, 24
coordination, 10
corpus callosum, 59

correspondence set, 48
cortex, 58
cranial capacity, 36
Creole, 78
Cro-Magnon, 32-33
Cuna, 29

deafness, 39
deixis, 83
de Laguna, Grace, 24-26
deletion, 10
dental, 4, 67
derivation, 8
design features, 54-56
determiner, 69-79
developmental schedule, 38
dialect, 43
Diamond, A. S., 26-27
differentiation, 25, 67
Ding-dong theory, 21
directive function, 17
discontinuity theories, 38
discourse unit, 17
displacement, 55
discreteness, 55
distinctive feature, 6
divergence, 45-46
diversification, 43
diversity, 41
dominance, hemispheric, 33,
    60-62
duality of patterning, 55
Durbin, Marshall, 50-51

embedding, 39
empiricist, 20
encapsulation, 56
eolithic, 28
Ervin-Tripp, Susan, 17, 74
expressive function, 15, 23

facultative expression, 9
family tree, 44